You Shall Surely Rejoice

You Shall Surely Rejoice

By:

Fr Kyrillos Farag

ST SHENOUDA PRESS
SYDNEY, AUSTRALIA
2025

YOU SHALL SURELY REJOICE
By: Fr Kyrillos Farag

COPYRIGHT © 2025
St. Shenouda Press

All rights reserved. Except for brief quotations in critical publications or reviews, no part of this book may be reproduced in any manner without prior written permission from the publisher.

ST SHENOUDA PRESS
8419 Putty Rd,
Putty, NSW, 2330
Sydney, Australia

www.stshenoudapress.com

ISBN 13: 978-1-7638415-0-5

All scripture quotations, unless otherwise indicated, are taken from the New King James Version®. Copyright © 1982 by Thomas Nelson, Inc. Used by permission. All rights reserved.

CONTENTS

Acknowledgments 1
Dedication 3
Introduction 5
Preface 7

Chapter 1.   Joy is Embedded in the Depths of intimate Relationship with Christ 11

Chapter 2.   Have you tasted The Transformative Power of Joy in your Life? 29

Chapter 3.   The Path to True Joy 41

Chapter 4.   Rejoicing with Christ's Joy: The Call to True Joy 55

Chapter 5.   What is the source of Joy 69

Chapter 6.   The Joy of Salvation 81

Chapter 7.   Joyful Service, the Heartbeat of Christian Ministry 97

Chapter 8.   Living in the Spirit: The Path to Joy through Love 113

Chapter 9.   A Glimpse of Eternal Joy in the Radiant Transfiguration 129

Chapter 10. Rejoicing in Hope, The Anchor of the Soul 147

Chapter 11.	Rejoicing in Submission and Simplicity: Lessons from the Life of Saint Mary	163
Chapter 12.	Savouring Joy in Suffering: Insights from Psalm 34	177
Chapter 13.	Embracing Joy in the midst of tribulations	189
Chapter 14.	The Paradox of Joy amid Suffering	197
Chapter 15.	Braving the Obstacles to Christian Joy	207
Chapter 16.	Cultivating true Joy—the way of Humility, Prayer and Repentance	221
Chapter 17.	Joy had been hiding in the tomb	235
Chapter 18.	The Fulness of Joy in His Presence	247
Chapter 19.	The Joy of Being Forgiven	263
Closing Words		275

ACKNOWLEDGMENTS

I would like to express my sincere gratitude to my dear Father, Daoud Lamie, who graciously accepted to introduce our work. His words are truly an honour to my humble book.

A special thank you goes to my dear Father, Anthony Saint Shenouda, whose vision led to the realisation of this book during one of our heartfelt conversations at the Monastery of Saint Shenouda the Archimandrite in Putty, NSW Australia.

We extend our deepest gratitude to the dedicated sisters and servants of the Lord, Mervette Attia and Tasony Mervat Attia. This book would not have come to fruition without their tireless efforts and hard work.

I extend my heartfelt thanks to Dr. Wagdy Samir and Janet Botros for their invaluable review of this material. Dr. Samir's insightful feedback and Janet Botros's meticulous suggestions have greatly enhanced this work. Their contributions have been crucial, and I am deeply appreciative of their support.

And finally, I extend my deepest appreciation and gratitude to Dr. Anna Silvas for her invaluable support in editing this work. Her profound expertise in the teachings of the Greek Fathers and the Christian East, particularly through her studies in Syriac/Aramaic, has significantly shaped my book. Anna's unique blend of scholarly insight, prayerful spirit, and delightful humour has enriched this journey in countless ways. Her influence is woven throughout these pages.

We would also like to thank all those who have provided their wisdom, support, and encouragement, enriching this endeavour and allowing us to share in the transformative power of Christ's joy.

DEDICATION

To the cherished memory of His Holiness Pope Shenouda III, whose radiant spirit and joyful heart illuminated

our path as we explored Christian joy. His profound life of unwavering faith, great wisdom, and boundless joy continues to inspire and guide us on our journey.

INTRODUCTION

"You shall surely rejoice"
Deut 16:15

Spiritual joy is simply the fruit of a real spiritual life. So, anyone who loves the living and true God and loves humankind through God, will bring forth spiritual fruits, especially the fruit of joy.

There are many kinds and expressions of something like joy in this life, but spiritual joy is different. It surpasses them all. It has nothing to do with wealth, health, or achievements. Spiritual joy is about faith, hope and love.

When you trust in God your Father, and you believe in His only begotten Son, the Redeemer and the giver of eternity through His resurrection, and when you trust in the work of the Holy Spirit in your heart, then you shall surely rejoice.

When you have earnest hope in the Word of God and you rely totally on His promises, you shall surely rejoice.

When you love God with all your heart, and with all your mind and with all your strength, and you love your fellow human beings as yourself, then you shall surely rejoice.

We need to embrace this joyful life in Christ, even in times of suffering and hardships, not only because it is God's commandment but also His Gift.

I am really honoured to introduce this precious book written and designed by my dear father, brother, and friend Abouna Kyrillos who had been always a man of God and a joyful person.

May God give you—the reader—the spirit of joy when you enjoy all the answers given to the frequent questions related to this important aspect of our spiritual life.

May our Lord Jesus Christ bless all the services and missions delivered by Father Kyrillos Farag.

With love
Revered Father Daoud Lamei

PREFACE

In a world increasingly driven by the pursuit of momentary pleasures and transient happiness, the experience of true joy often seems elusive and ever more distant. Yet, there is a profound and enduring joy that transcends the fleeting experiences of everyday life—one that is deeply rooted in our intimate relationship with our Lord Jesus Christ. "You Shall Surely Rejoice" is offered as a timely and insightful exploration of this divine joy, delving into its depths, its transformative power, and the ways it can sustain us through life's trials and tribulations.

I felt a deep passion to begin the journey of authoring this book, aiming to encourage and inspire my fellow brothers and sisters in Christ to embrace the joy that is offered to us. Despite life's challenges, I believe that choosing joy makes a profound difference.

It is indeed ironic that the people who have inspired me most, whether on the journey of writing this book or during my own moments of weakness in a turbulent life, have experienced traumatic events such as illness, the loss of loved ones, and carrying heavy ongoing burdens. This teaches us that joy and sorrow can coexist, and that joy can be born out of demanding situations. It is not for us to question or overanalyse how it emerges but rather to see it as part of how God operates in a way that surpasses our comprehension and imagination.

This book embarks on a heartfelt mission to unravel the complexities of joy, acknowledging that there is no single straightforward answer. Joy is not a fleeting emotion or a mere superficial feeling; it is a transformative force that emanates from a humble submission to the Lord and a faithful journey of learning, obedience, worship, praise, and gratitude. The beauty of joy lies in its availability and presence all around us, even amidst the challenges and obstacles that life presents.

Drawing inspiration from the Holy Scriptures, the wisdom of the desert fathers, and the experiences of faithful people, "You Shall Surely Rejoice" encourages us to live a joyful and victorious life here on earth, knowing that it continues in the everlasting joy of heaven. Through the gift of the Holy Spirit, we are reminded that joy becomes woven into our daily lives, empowering us to overcome anything that seeks to diminish it.

The chapters that follow delve into the multifaceted nature of joy, drawing from scriptural teachings, personal testimonies, and the wisdom of revered saints. From the parables of our Lord Jesus to the writings of Saint Paul, from the experiences of King David to lessons from Saint Mary, each chapter is a step towards unlocking and understanding how true joy can permeate our lives. We will explore joy's ability to coexist with suffering, its role in our spiritual growth, and its profound impact on our service to others.

As you embark on this transformative journey, dear reader, may this book serve as an invitation to question the presence of joy in your own life and to challenge and motivate you to live joyfully, as mandated and promised to us by God. Reflecting on the famous verse about joy in the book of Nehemiah, "the joy of the Lord is your strength," let us find strength, comfort, and reward in the ever-present joy accompanying our faith.

To deepen your engagement with the material and the pathway for joy, we have included a final word summary and a set of self-examining questions at the end of each chapter that we humbly offer for your reflection. These questions are designed to prompt introspection and encourage you to apply the principles discussed to your own life.

Whether you are seeking consolation in times of sorrow, strength in moments of weakness, or a deeper connection with your faith, this book aims to provide insights and reflections that will guide you towards the true joy that only our Lord Jesus Christ can offer. Let us embark on this journey together with open hearts and a spirit ready to embrace the divine joy that is our birthright as children of God. May the blessings of God be upon you as you embark on this joy-filled adventure. I humbly ask for your prayers and ongoing support as I present this book to you.

    Fr Kyrillos Farag

    16 June 2024

    The Feast of Ascension

Chapter 1

Joy is Embedded in the Depths of intimate Relationship with Christ

> *"Joy is the serious business of heaven."*
> Saint Gregory of Nyssa

How do you describe joy?

Describing the taste of a specific fruit to someone who has never tasted it is a challenging, if not impossible, task. Take, for instance, a mango or an orange. How can you truly describe their unique flavours? A mango combines sweet, mellow, and slightly tangy notes with a hint of floral undertones. An orange, on the other hand, offers a bright, zesty sweetness with a refreshing tang. Even these descriptions fall short of capturing a glimpse of the authentic taste experience.

Likewise, how do you describe a particular emotion to someone who has never experienced it? For instance, how can you describe being wretchedly poor to the rich in this world? A wealthy person cannot grasp what it means to sleep homeless at night without eating or without a blanket to protect you from the harsh winter, or to stare out the window of a clothing store, not daring even to think about buying a jacket to protect you from the harshness of weather.

Allow me to embark on this literary journey with you, dear reader, as we delve into the inexplicable depths of joy. Joy is a riddle that perplexes us, for how can one truly describe an emotion that eludes the grasp of those who have never experienced it? As I set foot on this path, I quickly realised that the challenging task that lies ahead of me is as formidable as it is rewarding.

Let me make one thing clear from the beginning: an answer to the question of joy can hardly be encompassed within a single chapter or a mere paragraph. Instead, it will reveal itself gradually through the compilation of each chapter, through the melodies of every verse, through the tapestry of each story, and through the whispers of prayer that have graced every page since I began to draft this book. We shall uncover the true essence of joy little by little illuminating the pathway to a life infused with its radiant light.

In this quest, I invite you to join me as we navigate the labyrinth of human emotions, exploring the boundless reaches of the human spirit. Together, we shall seek to understand the multifaceted nature of joy, for it is not a singular entity but a tapestry woven from various threads of experience, perception, and connection.

Joy is Embedded in the Depths of intimate Relationship with Christ

Throughout our journey, we shall encounter tales of triumph and resilience, anecdotes of profound love and of deep-seated gratitude, and reflections on moments of pure bliss that transcend the mundane. We shall delve into the wisdom of sages, the insights of poets, and the revelations of those who have walked this path before us.

So, dear reader, ready yourself for the adventure that lies ahead. Open your heart and mind to the possibility that joy is not an elusive mirage but a tangible reality that can be embraced and cultivated. Prepare to be captivated, challenged, and transformed as we navigate the pages of this book, for within its words lies the potential to unlock the secrets of a truly joyful existence. Describing God's joy to someone who has never experienced it is a challenging task, since it is a spiritual and transcendent concept. However, here is one attempt to describe it:

It is a state of perfect and unending bliss that emanates from God's very essence. Unlike human and this-worldly happiness, which can be affected by external circumstances.

The joy of God is rooted in His infinite love and perfect nature. It is a joy surpassing all understanding and human comprehension. It is a deep and profound satisfaction that comes from the fulfilment of His divine purposes and the perfect harmony within His creation.

The joy of God is not dependent on earthly pleasures or achievements but is wells up from His own eternal and unchanging nature. It is a joy that transcends time and space, encompassing all of

THE JOY OF GOD IS AN ETERNAL AND BOUNDLESS EXPRESSION OF DIVINE HAPPINESS AND DELIGHT.

creation, flowing from His love for all creation, from the beauty of His creation, and from the restoration and redemption of humanity.

> ❋
> GOD'S JOY IS CONSTANT AND UNCHANGING.

The joy of God is reflected in His relationship with us, His children. It is the joy that He feels when His children find their purpose, realise their full potential in accordance with His will, and experience true happiness.

While it may be difficult to fully grasp God's joy without experiencing it firsthand, this joy that is available to all who seek a genuine relationship with God. Through faith, prayer, and a deepening understanding of His love and forgiveness, one can begin to experience hints of God's joy in one's own life.

The journey of a new book

Embarking on the journey of drafting a new book is similar to stepping into uncharted territory. As it were, the beginning is the threshold between author and reader, a delicate exchange of words that sets the tone for what lies ahead. As I wondered how to captivate readers' attention, particularly as we delve into the profound realm of Christian joy, I found myself searching for a touching story—a tale of genuine joy that would resonate deeply with the human spirit. Despite my efforts, I found myself at an impasse, unable to think of a suitable narrative. It was then that I turned inward, drawing upon my experiences and reflections on individuals whose lives embodied the essence of joy.

Joy is Embedded in the Depths of Intimate Relationship with Christ

In this introspective journey, my thoughts inevitably turned to the revered figure of His Holiness Pope Shenouda III, may the Lord repose his pure soul, grant him eternal peace, and may we all receive his prayers for all of us before the Throne of God.

Amidst the weight of his papal responsibilities and the multitudinous challenges he faced, Pope Shenouda III radiated a profound sense of joy that left an unfading impression on all who crossed his path. His infectious smile, witty humour, and profound serenity amid adversity served as a beacon of hope and inspiration for Coptic communities worldwide. With each radiant expression and heartfelt prayer, Pope Shenouda exemplified the enduring power of Christian joy—a joy that transcends earthly trials because it finds its source in the boundless love of God.

Thus, with a sense of reverence and gratitude to this godly Father, I embark on this literary odyssey, weaving together insights gleaned from personal reflections, timeless wisdom, and the rich tapestry of Christian tradition. As we journey together, may we discover anew the transformative power of joy, as exemplified by the life and legacy of Pope Shenouda III, and may our hearts be uplifted by the enduring promise of divine grace and redemption. May his inspiring and joyful spirit accompany us on this journey of pursuing and understanding Christian joy.

In the Gospels, our Lord Jesus Christ spoke little about joy, with 12-13 verses touching upon the subject. Most of these verses are found in the Gospel according to Saint John the Evangelist, particularly in the chapters on the Paraclete at the brink of his Passion. Some sayings are in the Gospel of Saint Luke. However, this scarcity of direct mentions does not mean that our Lord Jesus Christ did not emphasise joy; in fact, He spoke of it as a command.

Before delving into the depths of this book, take a moment to deeply ponder: What does the concept of joy truly entail?

Is it when my boss calls me and informs me that I am the employee of the year and is giving me a promotion, my own office, and a pay rise of $30,000? Is this true joy?

Or is it true joy when I have gatherings with family members I have not seen in ages who live in the USA, Canada, Egypt, or Australia? Meeting up with them in beautiful places, talking to them and catching up with them. Yes, it is a good feeling, but is this true joy?

Is it when I buy new clothes, a new watch, a new car—of course the latest model, and the best brand everyone admires and only I can afford? God has given me extra money, and I bought it, rode it, and felt happy. Is this true joy? Or is it when others praise my good character, my wisdom, my manners, my family, my house, and my life? Is this true joy?

Let us explore the essence of genuine and true joy.

Joy is remarkably different from happiness — although they may overlap. Happiness depends on circumstances; joy depends solely, entirely, and fully on God. This is this book's

> ✴
> HAPPINESS VANISHES WHEN LIFE TURNS TO THE OTHER SIDE AND SOMETIMES BECOMES PAINFUL; JOY, ON THE OTHER HAND, CONTINUES AND MAY EVEN GROW AND DEEPEN AMIDST SICKNESS, PAIN, AND VARIOUS HARDSHIPS AND PROBLEMS.

Joy is Embedded in the Depths of intimate Relationship with Christ

most important and paramount message one we will keep presenting to you, my dear reader.

Joy comes and blossoms from living an intimate, vital relationship with God. It comes from grasping that this world is only temporary and vanishing, and someday, we will be with God eternally. It comes from the fact that although we do not yet see God, we believe in Him, we obey Him, and we live for Him in glorious joy—because of Him (1 Peter 1:8).

Joy is found in our Lord and Saviour Jesus Christ, *"the author and finisher of our faith, who for the joy that was set before Him endured the cross, despising the shame, and has sat down at the right hand of the throne of God"* (Hebrews 12:2).

True joy, as we have touched upon, is therefore a complex and profound emotion. It transcends mere happiness, which often hinges on fragile and changing external circumstances. It delves into the very essence of our being. It is not a fleeting feeling but a state of being rooted in our relationship with our Lord Jesus Christ.

Consider the parable of the prodigal son. When the wayward son returns home, regretful, repentant, and humbled, his father's joy knows no bounds. It is not the son's return alone that brings joy; it is the restoration of their lost relationship.

SIMILARLY, OUR JOY IS INTIMATELY TIED TO OUR RELATIONSHIP WITH OUR LORD JESUS CHRIST, WHO IS THE SOURCE OF THE FULLNESS OF JOY.

Think about the moments in your life when you experienced true joy. It was the quiet peace that enveloped and wrapped you during prayer, or the overwhelming sense of gratitude and contentment you experienced when you witnessed a remarkable work of God in your life, or an encounter of selflessly serving someone who really needed help that exhausted you physically and emotionally! Such moments, often inexplicable and transcendent, are glimpses of the joy that flows from our relationship with our Lord Jesus Christ.

As we journey deeper into the essence of true joy, let us consider its foundation in the teachings of our Lord Jesus Christ. In the Sermon on the Mount, He proclaimed, *"Blessed are you when they revile and persecute you and say all kinds of evil against you falsely for My sake. Rejoice and be exceedingly glad, for great is your reward in heaven"* (Matthew 5:11-12). Here, we see that true joy is not dependent on external circumstances but rooted in our identity as followers of Christ.

Our understanding of joy is further enriched by the Apostle Saint Paul's teachings on the fruit of the Holy Spirit. In his letter to the Galatians, he writes, *"But the fruit of the Spirit is love, joy, peace, long-suffering, kindness, goodness, faithfulness, gentleness, self-control"* (Galatians 5:22-23). True joy, then, is a manifestation of the Holy Spirit's work within us, a fruit of our relationship with our Lord Jesus Christ.

Joy is Embedded in the Depths of intimate Relationship with Christ

The source of our joy

"Now may the God of hope fill you with all joy and peace in believing, that you may abound in hope by the power of the Holy Spirit." Romans 15:13

As we embark on this profound exploration in search of the elusive keys to a joyful life, we inevitably encounter obstacles that hinder our progress. These obstacles, dear reader, are inherent to our fallen human nature. We possess a remarkable inclination to take matters into our own hands, to rely solely on our won skills, abilities, and resources, disregarding the wisdom, guidance, and sovereignty of God. It is our innate desire to be in control so that anything that threatens this control can cause us great anxiety and discomfort.

It is true that as human beings, we possess a remarkable capacity to reason, problem-solve, and act. We strive to fix our problems and overcome challenges through our own efforts based on our own experience. However, in our relentless pursuit of self-sufficiency, we often neglect the wisdom of seeking guidance from our sovereign God.

In our quest for joy, we must recognise the limitations of our own understanding and power. By humbly acknowledging that we do not have all the answers, we open ourselves to the possibility of seeking divine intervention and leaning on the support of others. This does not diminish our agency or our ability to make choices and act, but allows us to tap into a wellspring of strength and wisdom beyond our own limited perspective.

As we navigate the complexities of life, we must learn to submit our ego-driven desire for control and to embrace the beauty of submitting to a higher power. By entrusting our challenges and aspirations to the divine, we invite a sense of peace, guidance, and transcendence into our lives. We discover an immense power in aligning our will with a greater purpose and submitting to the sovereignty of something beyond ourselves, the Most High God.

So, dear reader, let us not be deterred by our innate tendency to rely solely on our own strength. Instead, let us embrace the transformative power of submit, allowing ourselves to be guided by the divine and supported by the loving presence of those around us. In this submit, we may find the clarity, peace, and joy that eluded us in our solitary conquest.

Once upon a time, on a breathtakingly sunny day in the vast expanse of Sydney's blue skies, I found myself consumed by the brave and eager spirit of a pilot-in-training. It was a dream I had nurtured throughout my whole life, but, in my younger years, I had never had the opportunity to fulfil it. Fuelled by determination, I embarked on a remarkable journey to learn the art of flying.

As I delved into the world of aviation, I encountered numerous lessons and challenges. Each experience was a stepping stone towards realising my dream. However, one particular lesson stood out from the rest, proving to be the most challenging and most daunting of them all: recovering a plane from stalling.

Stalling occurs when the angle of attack of an aircraft's wings exceeds the critical limit, leading to a loss of lift and potentially to a loss of control. It is a critical situation that demands quick thinking, precise actions, and unwavering composure. Learning how to recover from a stall is a crucial

Joy is Embedded in the Depths of intimate Relationship with Christ

skill for every pilot, as it can mean the difference between life and death.

As I faced this formidable lesson, I felt a mixture of trepidation and excitement. The gravity of the situation was not lost on me, but I was determined to conquer this daunting prospect and emerge as a skilled aviator. Under the guidance of experienced instructors, I learned the intricacies of recognising and responding to an impending stall.

The process involved a delicate balance of smoothly reducing the angle of attack, applying corrective measures, and regaining control of the aircraft. It required a deep understanding of aerodynamics, precise control inputs, and the ability to remain calm under pressure. Each attempt brought me steadily closer to mastering this vital skill.

But it was not without its moments of uncertainty and doubt. There were times when my heart raced, and my palms grew sweaty as I grappled with the complexities of recovering from a stall.

BUT WITH EACH CHALLENGE I FACED, I GREW MORE RESILIENT AND DETERMINED. I FACED DOWN THE FEAR AND TRANSFORMED IT INTO A DRIVING FORCE THAT PUSHED ME TOWARDS EXCELLENCE.

To master this essential skill, my dear reader, I simply had to intentionally initiate a stall by idling the propeller—hence no power and no lift—and gently upping the nose of the plane. Within seconds, the stalling initiated would send shivers down your spine. It was truly frightening as the small one-propellor plane on which you train began to dive. For a few seconds, you feel suspended and weightless as the nose dips down. You lose airspeed to the point where the plane cannot maintain its elevation but dives and baffles to the sound of some frightening alarms. But at that moment, you must act with very calm nerves and adequately, just as you have been trained.

Amidst the anxiety and pressure of this challenge, I had to save the situation by swiftly regaining control of the aircraft. I would do this by simply reintroducing power, at which point the nose tips over, and you regain airspeed again. But on that particular day, fear gripped my heart, rendering me unable to act as I should have. Control slipped through my fingers, and panic took hold.

In that moment of helplessness and inadequacy, when I was incapable of controlling the situation, something remarkable happened. I realised that a few inches right beside me sat an experienced instructor and pilot with a wealth of knowledge, a substantial number of flying hours, and expertise. Instead of solely focusing on my own perceived shortcomings and failures, I shifted my attention to the presence of my South American instructor. As is customary in flying, I said, "handing over," and the instructor acknowledged me by saying, "taking over." This protocol, followed in aviation between the pilot and copilot, ensures the utmost safety measures and avoids confusion that could lead to catastrophic events in such a high-stakes industry.

Like an angel of hope, my instructor pilot began to joyfully sing and whistle, bringing solace and comfort into the situation as he smoothly and instantly corrected the situation. At that moment, I had no choice but to trust in the expertise and guidance of my instructor, knowing that amid the risks of this flight, I was not alone. As my focus shifted from my own limitations to the steady presence of the instructor sitting a few inches next to me in the narrow cockpit of the Piper Aircraft, a renewed sense of calm washed over me.

At that moment, I discovered a profound lesson that extended far beyond the realm of flying. I realised that in life, losing control can be incredibly daunting and leave us feeling anxiously and desperately helpless. But just as I found solace in my instructor, so too we can find comfort and guidance in our greatest instructor and protector: God. Handing over to God is the key to handling all our challenges in life.

Just as I learned to trust in my instructor's expertise, so we too are encouraged to place our trust in God, who is always by our side, always in complete control of the journey of our life and say handing over to the Lord everything that we cannot deal with or find a solution. And God, accordingly, will always respond by taking over.

When we redirect our focus from our own limitations to the unwavering presence of God, a sense of warm, radiant, and joyful peace and reassurance follows that encapsulates our hearts.

This inspiring story serves as a reminder that no matter how turbulent life may become, we can find solace and strength in trusting God, our ultimate instructor. By submitting our fears and uncertainties to Him, we can navigate the challenges that come our way with a renewed sense of hope and confidence.

In our quest to cultivate true joy, we must also acknowledge our challenges and obstacles. The Apostle Saint Peter reminds us, *"In this you greatly rejoice, though now for a little while, if need be, you have been grieved by various trials"* (1 Peter 1:6). True joy does not exempt us from suffering; rather, it sustains us through it, offering hope and resilience in the face of adversity. I invite you to think and meditate on the above verse of Saint Peter. It is the unwavering

JOY IS NOT A FLEETING EMOTION BUT A DEEP-SEATED CONFIDENCE IN GOD'S PROVIDENCE AND CARE.

belief that God controls every aspect of our lives, even when circumstances seem hazardous and uncertain. This settled assurance allows us to face life's difficulties with a sense of peace and trust in God's goodness and produce divine joy.

As we navigate the complexities of life, let us hold fast to the promise of true joy in our Lord Jesus Christ – and again, I repeat—in Him only. This is not a fleeting emotion tied to

Joy is Embedded in the Depths of intimate Relationship with Christ

temporary pleasures but the sense of a deep and abiding presence that sustains us through every trial and triumph.

> "Joy is the settled assurance that God is in control of all the details of my life, the quiet confidence that ultimately everything is going to be alright, and the determined choice to praise God in every situation."
> Max Lucado

Joy is characterised by a quiet, steadfast confidence in God's faithfulness. It is the inner assurance that, no matter what trials or tribulations we may face, God is working all things together for our good. This quiet confidence enables us to navigate the storms of life with grace and resilience, knowing that God is with us every step of our life's journey.

Furthermore, Joy is also a conscious decision, indeed, a very conscious decision to praise God in every situation, regardless of our circumstances. It is choosing to focus on God's righteousness, goodness, and faithfulness rather than dwelling on our problems or struggles. This determined choice to praise God is not contingent on our feelings or external circumstances but upon trust, belief and confidence in God's promises and provision. At the core of joy is the unwavering belief in God's sovereignty over all things and at all times. It is the deeply rooted understanding that God is in control and that His plans for us are good and purposeful. This confidence in God's sovereignty allows us to submit our worries and fears, knowing that He is working all things according to His perfect will.

The essence of true joy is beautifully captured in the words of the Psalmist, who declares, *"You will show me the path of life; At Your right hand are pleasures forevermore"* (Psalm 16:11). Here, we find that true joy is not found in fleeting pleasures or material possessions but in the presence of our Lord Jesus Christ. It is a joy that transcends the circumstances of our lives and fills us with a profound sense of peace and contentment.

> ❋
> "IN YOUR PRESENCE IS FULLNESS OF JOY;

Throughout the Scriptures, we find numerous examples of individuals who experienced true joy in their relationship with God. From the exuberant praise of King David dancing before the Ark to the steadfast faith of Job amid suffering, these stories remind us that true joy does not depend on our external circumstances but on our intimate connection with our Lord Jesus Christ.

In the New Testament, we see how the early Christians were filled with true and authentic joy even in the face of oppression, adversity, and hardships. The Apostle Saint Paul, writing from prison, encouraged the Philippians to *"rejoice in the Lord always"* (Philippians 4:4), demonstrating that true joy is not dependent on our surroundings but on our relationship with our Lord Jesus Christ.

As believers and followers of Christ, we are called to cultivate a deep and abiding joy of heart that springs from our relationship with Him. This joy is not based on our own efforts or achievements but on the unchanging love and grace of our Lord Jesus Christ. It is a joy that sustains us through the trials and tribulations of life, filling us with hope and peace even in the darkest of times.

In the words of the Apostle Saint Paul, *"May the God of hope fill you with all joy and peace as you trust in Him, so that you may overflow with hope by the power of the Holy Spirit"* (Romans 15:13). Let us, therefore, fix our eyes on our

Lord Jesus Christ, the author and perfecter of our faith, and allow His joy to fill our hearts and lives.

To conclude, then: true joy is not found in the fleeting pleasures of this world but in our relationship with our Lord Jesus Christ. It is a joy that transcends circumstances and fills us with a deep and abiding peace. May we, as followers of Christ, experience the fullness of this joy and share it with others as we journey together in faith.

Final words

The first Chapter of this book focussed on the concept of true joy, exploring joy as a natural affect resonating from a deep relationship with our Lord and Saviour, Jesus Christ. Joy is different from passing happiness since it depends on God rather than external circumstances. True joy is found in a living and vital relationship with God, knowing that this world is temporary and we are called to be with Him forever. It is a complex and profound emotion that transcends transient feelings and is rooted in our connection with our Lord Jesus.

The chapter has emphasised that true joy is intimately tied to our relationship with our Lord Jesus Christ, as seen in the parable of the prodigal son and teachings from the Sermon on the Mount. It also discusses joy as a manifestation of the Holy Spirit's work within us and acknowledges that true joy does not exempt us from suffering but sustains us through it with hope and resilience. The chapter concludes by emphasising that true joy is a settled assurance in God's control over our lives, a conscious decision to praise God in every situation, and an unwavering belief in God's sovereignty.

Questions for self-reflection:

1. How do you currently define joy in your life?

2. What moments have you experienced true joy in your relationship with God?

3. How does your understanding of joy differ from happiness?

4. In what ways do external circumstances impact your joy? How can you cultivate a joy rooted in God rather than circumstances?

5. How does your relationship with our Lord Jesus Christ contribute to your experience of true joy?

6. How do you navigate challenges and obstacles in your life while maintaining a sense of joy?

7. What role does trust in God's providence and sovereignty play in your experience of joy?

8. How can you cultivate a deeper and abiding joy in your relationship with our Lord Jesus Christ?

9. Are there any areas in your life where you are seeking joy from temporary pleasures or material possessions rather than from your relationship with God?

10. How can you share the joy you have experienced with others and encourage them in their own journey of faith and eternal life?

Chapter 2

Have you tasted The Transformative Power of Joy in your Life?

"Let us always guard our souls against despondency and sorrow, for it leads to spiritual death."
Saint John Chrysostom

Is joy a choice that we can make?

Have you ever wondered if joy is truly within our control? Do you grasp, my dear reader, the above question? Is joy an option that we can actively choose to embrace joy? Can we cultivate it? Is it a mindset? Many questions arose in my mind while approaching the second chapter of this book. I must admit that the title of this book, "You Shall Surely Rejoice," keeps challenging me. It has sparked a deep curiosity within me and ignited a passionate questioning about the authenticity and relevance of joy in my life. I keep wrestling with the idea in my heart, soul, and mind. On the one hand, I like working, thinking, and writing about joy. On the other hand, I pray all the time that the book in your hands may be an authentic book with a liveable message; I hope that it will open our eyes, dear readers, to the diminishing treasure of joy in our lives, to see that it is fading slowly and disappearing from our world especially among us Christian believers.

Yes, joy can be a choice that we can make. While we may not always have control over the circumstances or events that occur in our lives, we do have a choice in how we respond to them because joy is not essentially dependent on external factors but is rather a state of mind and an attitude that we can and are called to cultivate.

Choosing joy does not mean denying or suppressing our emotions, especially during times of sorrow or hardship. It means actively seeking and embracing the positive aspects of life, even amid challenges. It involves focusing on gratitude, finding meaning and purpose in our earthly journey, and nurturing a hopeful outlook.

By choosing joy, we shift our perspective and mindset, allowing ourselves to experience moments of happiness and contentment, even in difficult circumstances. It is not always easy, and it may require intentional effort and practice, but

MAKING THE CONSCIOUS DECISION TO CHOOSE JOY CAN HAVE A TRANSFORMATIVE IMPACT ON OUR OVERALL WELL-BEING.

Have you tasted The Transformative Power of Joy in your Life?

Joy embraces both external circumstances and our internal response to them. While we cannot control everything that happens to us, we can choose how we approach and navigate life's unavoidable ups and downs. By choosing joy, we empower ourselves to find light in darkness and to cultivate a greater sense of peace and fulfilment. Let us explore this challenge in a deeper context.

Joy and sorrow can coexist

I would love to share with you a profound lesson I gained from a true story that I have come across. It has profoundly impacted my understanding of love, faith, and transformation. To respect the privacy and identity of the beautiful couple involved, I have altered the names and some details, but the essence of their journey, as told here, remains. This story highlights the remarkable power of faith and commitment in overcoming personal and relational obstacles, and it serves as an inspiring testament to the strength that can be found in unity and divine guidance.

Mark and Emily had always dreamed of starting a family together. After years of struggling with infertility, they finally received the exciting news they had been longing for: Emily was pregnant, and not only that, but pregnant with twins. Their joy knew no bounds as they eagerly prepared for the arrival of their twin babies.

However, their happiness was soon overshadowed by unforeseen complications during childbirth. Despite all the efforts of the medical team, one of their twins, Lily, passed away shortly after birth. The loss was devastating, leaving Mark and Emily grappling with grief and heartache.

Amid their pain, Mark and Emily found unexpected moments of joy and comfort. They were overwhelmed by the outpouring of love and support from their family, friends, and the church community. Acts of kindness, heartfelt messages, and gestures of empathy were reminders that they were not alone in their sorrow.

Amidst their grief, Mark and Emily drew strength from their faith, finding solace in the belief that Lily's life, though so brief, had a purpose and meaning. They cherished the precious memories they had created with their daughter, holding onto the joy she had brought into their lives, however fleeting it may have been.

As they navigated the difficult journey of grief and healing, Mark and Emily discovered that joy and sorrow could coexist. While their hearts ached for the loss of Lily, they also found moments of joy in the presence of their surviving twin, Noah. His laughter, smiles, and milestones became sources of light in their darkest days. Through their experience, Mark and Emily learned that joy is not about the absence of pain but about embracing all of life's moments—joyful and the sorrowful—with courage, resilience, and gratitude. Their journey taught them that even in the face of loss, love endures, and

JOY CAN BE FOUND IN THE MOST UNEXPECTED PLACES.

Today, Mark and Emily honour Lily's memory by cherishing every moment they have with Noah and finding joy in the simple pleasures of life. Their journey of grief and healing has deepened their appreciation for the gift of life and the resilience of the human spirit and empowered them to help and support other people in their community who might experience adversity and sorrows. They chose to move forward in strength and resilience through their faith.

> "In the day when I cried out, You answered me,
> And made me bold with strength in my soul."
> (Psalm 138)

At some point in life, we all feel the loneliness of sorrow. Mary and Martha were saddened by the death of their brother, Lazarus, and Martha said to our Lord Jesus, "If you had been here, my brother would not have died." Theirs was a loneliness of sorrow. The shortest verse in the Scriptures tells us that at the tomb of Lazarus, "Jesus wept." This shows that He understands our pain and enters our sorrows. *"In all their affliction He was afflicted"* (Isaiah 63:9). Just think about this and reflect for a moment that He walks with us, He carries our burdens, He feels with our pain and sorrow and is afflicted with our afflictions. God does not keep watching us from a remote distance and feel sorry for us from afar off, but stoops down, engages, participates, and is afflicted by our afflictions.

> GOD FEELS, UNDERSTANDS, AND KNOWS ALL OUR AFFLICTION, AND NOT ONLY KNOWS IT, BUT ENTERS IT WITH US.

We all feel sad sometimes because we are human, but long-term sadness is unsuitable for you. It affects you physically which is why many people wonder why their heart hurts. What makes you sad so much of the time? People struggle with so many distinct aspects of this life. Yes, there are many causes for sorrow – yet God offers us hope. Scripture says, *"The Lord is near to those who have a broken heart, And saves such as have a contrite spirit."* (Psalm 34:18)

When we come to our Lord Jesus Christ, He does not promise to exempt us from trouble or sorrow. Tears will surely come, but deep inside, there will be a joy that is difficult to explain in words. It is a joy from God — the effect of the Holy Spirit. Amid trials, agony, and tears that come to us all, supernatural power is poured out, bringing forth joy.

In our journey through life, we often encounter moments of trial and adversity. During these challenging times, the true power of joy becomes evident. Despite the turmoil and uncertainty that may surround us, God grants us an interior joy that serves as a source of strength, resilience, and power.

But what exactly do we mean when we speak of joy as power? Everything in the universe has transformative potential. What can energize this transformation? What has the power to do so? Love has an enormous power to work miracles. Forgiveness, too, has incredible power to reconcile, mend and restore broken relationships. Similarly, joy comes imbued with its own unique power—a divine force to sustain and uplift us even in the darkest of times.

The joy of the Lord is our strength

We find a profound illustration of the power of joy in the Old Testament story of Nehemiah. Confronted with the rubble of Jerusalem, Nehemiah nevertheless vowed to rebuild the city's ruined walls. Despite facing innumerable obstacles and challenges, he found favour in the eyes of king Artaxerxes and received permission to undertake this monumental task.

In the book of Nehemiah (chapter 8:1-10), we witness a poignant moment as Ezra, the scribe, reads from the Book of the Law before the assembly of people. Initially, the people weep as they hear the words of the Law and are confronted with their sins. Yet, Nehemiah reassures them, declaring, *"Do not sorrow, for the joy of the LORD is your strength"* (Neh 8:10). This verse in the context encapsulates a profound truth: Even in moments of sorrow and deep repentance, God grants us words of comfort and joy, strengthening us to face whatever lies ahead.

TRUE JOY IS NOT CONTINGENT ON OUR EXTERNAL CIRCUMSTANCES BUT IS ROOTED IN OUR RELATIONSHIP WITH GOD.

This is the joy that we want to feel, to be saturated and engulfed in, the true joy, not the poor substitutes we seek to find in other things, the worldly joy. It is the interior joy from within our hearts that the Holy Spirit pours out in us, the joy that lasts and which no one can take from you, the joy that comes from God and from His presence in our hearts. The joy that comes from God supports us and gives us the power to continue our path to eternity, to heaven, to the kingdom, that has been prepared for and promised to us, not becoming waylaid with problems and challenges, not focussing on the obstacles alone, not seeing the negatives in people or in the world, because we know true joy, the interior joy.

When no joy exists in our hearts, we become easily annoyed. Anything can set us off; truly, little pleases us, and we become hyper-critical, always seeing the wrong in others. Nothing satisfies us. This mindset becomes reflected in our words, our lack of gratitude and appreciation of others, our nagging and complaining.

In contrast, the person who has joy in their heart does not focus on the faults of others, gives thanks for the work of God, is easily pleased, has eyes that see God's beautiful creation, sees the good in others, and has compassion on others. This is quite a different point of view to someone without joy because the lens with which they view life is a heart full of the fruit of the Holy Spirit, which comes from a deep relationship with our Lord Christ. Then, the Holy Spirit pours upon them joy and rest and the fruit of the Spirit. The frustrated person does not live according to God's plan.

God promised us abundant life

God does not want us to have a miserable life! He promised, *"I have come that they may have life, and that they may have it more abundantly"* (John 10:10), also, *"In Your presence is fullness of joy"* (Psalm 16:11). His plan for our life is that we be joyful, not miserable, *"That they may see your good works and glorify your Father in heaven"* (Matthew 5:16). Our Lord is saying that when others see that we are joyful and thankful, and not critical of others, they will glorify God. It becomes natural to live such a life of joy because this is the work of the Holy Spirit.

The journey from sorrow to joy is a recurring theme throughout the Scriptures. King David, in Psalm 30:11, rejoices in God's ability to turn mourning into dancing—a testament to the transformative power of joy in our lives.

Unlike the fleeting pleasures of the world, this true joy emanates from within our hearts. It is a gift bestowed upon us by the Holy Spirit—a joy that endures and cannot be taken away. As we immerse ourselves in God's presence, in church and in our hearts, we are enveloped in this divine joy that sustains us on our journey towards eternity.

The Apostle Saint Paul, in (Galatians 5:22), speaks of the fruit of the Spirit, emphasising joy as a manifestation of a life lived in communion with God. This joy, born out of our relationship with Christ, serves as a barometer of our spiritual vitality and union with God. When joy fills our hearts, it manifests itself in our words and actions. Our speech reflects the abundance of joy within us, echoing the sentiments of (Psalm 105:2,) *"Sing to Him, sing Psalms to Him; talk of all His wondrous works."*

Conversely, when joy is absent, our whole demeanour sours. We become critical and discontented, lacking in thanksgiving and full of complaints.

A heart filled with joy sees the world through a different lens—one characterised by compassion, gratitude, and steadfastness. This joy enables us to overcome hardships and difficulties with resilience and grace, knowing that our strength lies in the joy of the Lord *"for the joy of the LORD is your strength."* (Nehemiah 8:10)

As we navigate the complexities of life, let us choose joy—the joy that springs from an intimate relationship with Christ and is sustained by the Holy Spirit. For

Joy enables us to overcome the hardships and difficulties we face in our daily lives. In the book of Hebrews, we read, *"Looking unto Jesus... who for the joy that was set before Him endured the cross, despising the shame"* (Hebrews 12:2). This joy gives us the power to overcome the problems around us, it will continue, and life will continue too.

IT IS THIS JOY THAT EMPOWERS US TO FACE LIFE'S CHALLENGES WITH COURAGE AND FAITH, KNOWING THAT GOD IS WITH US EVERY STEP OF THE WAY.

Joy is available, it is your choice!

In our life, we always have two choices: either to live joyfully with whatever God gives us, just as Job said to his wife, *"The Lord gave, and the Lord has taken away; Blessed be the name of the Lord."* (Job 1:21). Or we can live in internal conflict, whinging, nagging, complaining, continuously feeling sad and sorry for ourselves, always prone to being irritated and upset. So, it is a choice. I sincerely believe that everything in our life is a choice! We can choose to have this joy which the Holy Spirit gives, *"For the joy of the LORD is your strength"* (Nehemiah 8:10). In summary, joy is a tremendously transformative power, a delightful fruit given to us by our Lord through the work of the Holy Spirit, so that we can carry on in our life in and through hardships. But remember, it is natural for one to be so transformed, the result of a strong, intimate relationship with Christ, crowned by the Holy Spirit who pours on us the fruit of the Spirit in our hearts.

My dear reader, we are all invited to live life in abundance of joy, contentment, and *"the peace of God which surpasses all understanding and guards our heart and mind in Christ Jesus"* (Philippians 4:7). Joy is our choice; it is available, secured and granted for us in our Lord Jesus Christ.

Final words

In this chapter, we delved into the profound impact of joy on our lives, exploring how it serves as a source of strength and resilience, even amidst trials and adversity. Through the experiences of individuals like Mark and Emily, who found moments of joy amidst profound loss, and biblical figures like Nehemiah, who exemplified the power of joy in the face of daunting challenges, we uncover the transformative nature of true joy—a divine force that sustains and uplifts us.

True joy possesses a transformative power that sustains us through life's inevitable trials and adversities. Unlike fleeting happiness, joy emanates from our relationship with God and can coexist with sorrow. Drawing from biblical examples and subjective experiences, we learn that It enables us to navigate life's complexities with courage, resilience, and gratitude, knowing that God's presence sustains us and empowers us to overcome obstacles.

JOY IS NOT CONTINGENT ON EXTERNAL CIRCUMSTANCES BUT SPRINGS FROM AN INTIMATE CONNECTION WITH OUR LORD CHRIST.

Questions for self-reflection:

1. Reflect on a time in your life when you experienced joy amidst adversity. How did this experience impact your perspective on challenges and difficulties?

2. Consider the story of Mark and Emily. How did they find moments of joy amid their grief? What lessons can we learn from their journey of healing and resilience?

3. Explore the biblical account of Nehemiah and the transformative power of joy in rebuilding the walls of Jerusalem. How does his story inspire you to find joy in facing the obstacles in your own life?

4. Think about the role of the Holy Spirit in cultivating joy in your life. How can you deepen your relationship with God to experience greater joy and resilience?

5. Consider the impact of joy on your words and actions. How does joy manifest in your interactions with others, especially during challenging times?

6. Reflect on the statement, "The joy of the Lord is your strength" (Nehemiah 8:10). How does this truth empower you to face life's challenges with courage and faith?

7. And finally, in what ways can you actively choose joy in your daily life, even amidst difficulties and hardships? What practical steps can you take to nurture a spirit of joyfulness rooted in your relationship with Christ.

Chapter 3

The Path to True Joy

"When spiritual joy comes to the body from the mind, it suffers no diminution by this communion with the body, but rather transfigures the body, spiritualising it—rejecting all evil desires of the flesh, it no longer weighs down the soul but rises up with it, the wholeperson becoming spirit." Saint Gregory Palamas

Let us redefine joy together!

Get ready to embark on a journey to redefine our understanding of joy. It is important for both of us, dear readers, to be on the same page and truly comprehend the essence of joy, especially as we explore the path to true joy.

Now, let us pause for a moment and ponder: What does true joy mean to you? When I mention true joy, what comes to mind? Do we have a shared understanding? Can you put it into words and explain it to someone? Can you describe how do you feel when you experience joy in your heart?

There is, however, a significant aspect to consider - our usual approach to defining joy often involves relying on external sources, such as dictionaries, or even my own previous tendency to mention it summarily as one of the fruits of the Holy Spirit. Nevertheless, today, we have the opportunity to break free from this conventional mould and explore a captivating definition of true joy that I came across during my research.

You see, part of the problem is that we have diminished joy as a mere synonym for happiness. But let me tell you, true joy is so much more than that! It is time to uncover the depths of joy that scripture reveals to us. Are you ready? Let us dive in! On his website, Word from the Word, Dr Dan Hayden writes:

"The key to our understanding the joy of the Lord, however, is to observe carefully the specific joy our Lord had in mind in His prayer. When our Lord Jesus prayed, He said, *"that they might have **my** joy fulfilled in themselves"* (John 17:13). There it is. Do you see it? He does not have **our** joy (in the sense of what pleases us) in mind at all. Rather, He is thinking of His own joy brought to completion (fulfilled) in our Christian lives. That is more than an interesting observation. It is the essence of knowing what the Bible means when it refers to Christian joy. The joy of the Lord, quite frankly, is the Lord's joy. In other words, it is the kind of joy He experienced when He was on the earth…. Our Lord is praying for us that we might have His joy fulfilled in us. What is He praying? He is praying that we will enter into such a close union with Him that the joy of His life will be the joy of our lives. He is praying that we will catch the vision of devoting our lives to the glory of God and to His purpose in the world with the realisation that we will one day share in His glory. Oh, what a joy it is—no matter the cost!" –Dr Dan Hayden."

Please keep this in mind, my dear reader, while reading this book that the true joy is the joy that our Lord and saviour Jesus Christ prayed to the father in the gospel of Saint John chapter 17. It is His joy, not our joy—quite a remarkable difference, isn't it? Now, let us unlock together the path to true joy and see where we have misstepped and stumbled in our life journey.

Lifetime lesson from the wisest king

King Solomon, the son of King David, ascended to the throne despite having six other brothers from different mothers. Bathsheba, the widow of Uriah the Hittite, bore Solomon, and David cherished him dearly as he was from his beloved wife.

King Solomon's name, meaning "man of peace" in Hebrew, resonated with King David's prayer for a peaceful reign. Remarkably, there were no wars during King Solomon's rule, a testament to his wisdom and diplomatic finesse. Sadly, by the end of his reign, King Solomon's heart had turned away from God.

He replaced the love of God and all the many blessings He had received from him with strange love; Solomon loved many foreign women, and, in the end, he had 700 wives and 300 concubines (1 Kings 11). Later he said about himself, "I made my works great, I built myself houses, and planted myself vineyards. I made myself gardens and orchards, and I *planted all kinds of fruit trees in them. I made myself water pools from which to water the growing trees of the grove. I acquired male and female servants I also gathered for myself silver and gold and the special treasures of kings and of the provinces and whatever my eyes desired I did not keep from them. Then I looked on all the works that my hands had done and on the labour in which I had toiled; And indeed, all was vanity and grasping for the wind. There was no profit under the sun"* (Ecclesiastes 2:2-11).

But early in Solomon's reign, God appeared to him in a dream, offering him any request. He humbly asked for wisdom, a request granted by God. His wisdom shone brightly in the famous case of the two disputing women, earning admiration from all quarters. Throughout his reign, King Solomon's wisdom was continually displayed and acknowledged.

One of King Solomon's greatest blessings was the opportunity to build the Temple, a testament to God's favour upon him. However, in the twilight of his reign, King Solomon's heart strayed from God's path. He succumbed to earthly desires, particularly his infatuation with foreign women, accumulating a staggering number of wives and concubines. In his introspection, King Solomon realised the futility of his pursuits, lamenting the vanity of earthly endeavours.

King Solomon's downfall serves as a cautionary tale against substituting fleeting pleasures in place of divine blessings. Often, we, too, are tempted to exchange true joy for transient satisfactions, leading to spiritual emptiness and distancing ourselves from God. But God's plan is not one of such replacements, such facile counterfeits; rather, The above quotation from Saint Gregory explores the concept of spiritual joy and its impact on the body. According to him, when spiritual joy emanates from the mind and enters the body, it does not diminish in any way. Instead, it transforms and spiritualises the body, freeing it from the weight of earthly desires.

HE DESIRES TO FILL OUR HEARTS WITH THE JOY THAT ENDURES.

Saint Gregory suggests that this communion between the mind and the body leads to a transfiguration of the entire person. Once burdened by sinful desires, the body is liberated and rises along with the soul. In this state, the person becomes more and more aligned with the spiritual realm, as indicated by the quote from the Gospel of John: *"He who is born of the Spirit is spirit."*

I will see you, and your heart will rejoice

In our Lord Jesus Christ's last words to his disciples before his Passion, he said, *"Most assuredly, I say to you that you will weep and lament, but the world will rejoice; and you will be sorrowful, but your sorrow will be turned into joy. A woman, when she is in labour, has sorrow because her hour has come; but as soon as she has given birth to the child, she no longer remembers the anguish, for joy that a human being has been born into the world. Therefore you now have sorrow; but I will see you again and your heart will rejoice, and your joy no one will take from you"* (John 16:19-22).

Consider the last verse in this passage, *"You now have sorrow; but I will see you again and your heart will rejoice, and your joy no one will take from you."* God gives gifts to everyone and reveals to us, "My aim and My plan is to give you joy," not an external joy, but a joy that comes from within the heart, and no one will take that joy from you unless you allow something to enter your heart and steal that joy away from you, and then, you lose that joy.

Our Lord Jesus knows and says, *"You have sadness."* He does not say replace the sadness, but the sadness itself will transform or turn into joy, (Psalm 30:11). Our Lord Christ, in every situation, will change it, transform it. He turns the darkness into light, transforms the tomb into resurrection, and changes the shame of the Cross into glory.

> ✳
> "You have turned for me my mourning into dancing"

This is our Lord Jesus. If we are going to replace what God has given us and provided for us, then we cannot reach God's plan and potential for our lives and will not experience true joy. Many looked for satisfaction, worldly fulfilment, and dreams of happiness, and in the end, none of this was obtained. Counterfeits and facile replacements are not in God's plan for us. Our Lord Jesus is changing and transforming us. He can replace the pain with something different, but afterwards, the sorrow of travail will be turned into the joy that a human being has been born into the world. He turns sadness into joy, and He transforms evil into good. Many ungodly people have been transformed into very righteous people, and many selfish people have been transformed into godly people.

We find reassurance in times of sorrow. Just as our Lord Jesus promised his disciples that their sorrow would be transformed into joy, so too can our sorrows be turned into rejoicing. Lord Jesus Christ's transformative power turns darkness into light and despair into hope, offering a pathway to lasting joy.

Are we replacing God with something else?

In the enchanting world of our childhood, my brother and I shared an extraordinary passion for collecting rare stamps. It was a delightful hobby that brought us closer together, igniting our curiosity and fuelling our imaginations. Each stamp told a story and held a piece of history from a faraway land. Over the years, our collection grew in size and beauty, as we received stamps as presents from our parents, relatives, and friends all over the world.

Our prized possession was carefully housed in numerous albums, each page adorned with stamps from different countries, commemorating events from special occasions in the United Nations to the first landing on the moon, reflecting many unique cultures and traditions. We cherished these albums, adding new stamps with every opportunity that came our way. The collection became a treasure trove, a testament to our dedication and love for the art of stamp collecting.

Time flew by, and as life unfolded, our visits to the collection became less and less frequent. Yet, whenever we found ourselves longing for a nostalgic journey, we would open the closet where the albums were kept and immerse ourselves in the memories they held. We would marvel at the vibrant colours, intricate designs, and the stories they whispered, and honestly, we forget about time as we relived those memorable moments from childhood.

But one fateful day, when we decided to revisit our beloved collection, we were met with a heart-wrenching surprise. As we opened the albums, our eyes widened in disbelief. The stamps that once adorned the pages had vanished, replaced by a sea of colourful stickers, the kind that came free with packets of snacks. Our astonishment knew no bounds, and a wave of disappointment crashed over us.

At that moment, we discovered the mischievous culprit behind this unexpected transformation - our little sister. At the time, she was just a young child attending early primary school, innocent and unaware of our stamps' immense value. In her innocence, she had exchanged our precious stamps with her friends in school and replaced them with those insignificant stickers that brought joy to her young heart.

Although our hearts sank, we could not be angry with our little sister. We realised that she was merely an innocent child, unable to comprehend the significance of our collection. It was a moment of understanding and forgiveness, as we recognised that sometimes, in our journey through life, we too make the mistake of replacing precious treasures with trivial and forgettable things from the world.

Have you ever considered this? In our lives, we often replace one thing with another. It is worth examining our hearts and relationship with God if we lack joy. "*But my people have exchanged their glorious God for worthless idols.*" (Jeremiah 2:11). Are we seeking substitutes for true fulfilment?

This might be why we do not experience genuine Godly joy. We hold on to God with one hand, while with the other we are busy seeking replacements. We try to balance, or I should call it more precisely compromise, but life with our Lord should be fulfilling, complete, and filled with joy. This is the true joy God wants us to experience, to taste, to understand, to live and immerse ourselves in.

Do not try to find out how we can acquire joy or what are the practical points or steps, as if it were some kind of technique. That is not how God operates or how Christianity works. It is the work of God. So, how can we put it into a series of practical, manipulable steps? It is not an app we can download to navigate our way to joy.

TRUE JOY IS THE MYSTERIOUS WORK OF THE HOLY SPIRIT, IT IS THE SECRET DIVINE WORK INSIDE THE HEART.

We may begin with our minds functioning in a worldly way. Still, as we progress in our life of faith and love and hope, our Lord Jesus becomes more and more our life, until we can say with St Paul, "*It is no longer I who live, but Christ lives in me*" (Galatians 2:20). So, when our Lord Jesus lives in us, He will fill us with joy, and His Holy Spirit grants us the fruits of the Spirit.

We risk our true fulfilment when we seek joy outside God's plan. Christianity is not about acquiring joy through practical steps but about submitting to the Holy Spirit's work within us. As we submit our lives to Jesus, His Spirit fills us, granting us the fruit of joy.

Do not trim God to our own limited perspectives

We must avoid framing and confining God to our own limited understanding, and least of all to our seeking joy through external means. God cannot be contained within the confines of our worldly perspectives! Attempting to seek him in this way only limits our experience of His boundless love and joy. We have rather to immerse ourselves in prayer, Scripture, and service to others, allowing Jesus to dwell within us and fill us with His abundant joy.

When we submit our entire lives to our Lord Jesus, inviting Him to reign in every aspect of our being, joy naturally and smoothly diffuses into our hearts through the presence and mysterious work of the Holy Spirit. It is not a question of seeking joy as an end goal but rather about submitting to God's will and allowing His joy to permeate every inch, every corner, and every fibre of our being. In our quiet moments of prayer, study of Scripture, and selfless acts of service, we open ourselves up to receive the fullness of God's joy.

Never attempt to frame God!

Sometimes, as humans, we try to fit God into our limited worldly understanding. We may try to define and understand God based on our own experiences and a very analytical style of thinking, the way we have been programmed within the learning system to become patterned-minded. By this we mean that we tend to put situations, people, circumstances, and experiences in life into frames and fixed templates. This is because our minds are finite, and we naturally seek to make sense of the world around us using the knowledge and concepts we are familiar with.

However, we must remember that God is beyond human comprehension and cannot be fully grasped or confined within our earthly understanding.

Avoid confining God to our limited perspectives. We sometimes impose our narrow experiences on Him, expecting Him to act within those boundaries. Do not frame God. Let us not confine God to our worldly understanding and the frameworks of our minds but instead open ourselves up to His transformative power. As we abide in Him, His joy becomes our strength, guiding us through life's challenges and illuminating our path with His eternal light. May God's joy overflow in our hearts as we embrace His plan for our lives.

Final words

This chapter delved into the story King Solomon's reign marked to begin with by wisdom and divine favour, and yet his heart strayed from God's path by succumbing to earthly desires, particularly his infatuation with foreign women. Despite his worldly accomplishments, King Solomon realises the futility of his pursuits, lamenting the vanity of earthly endeavours. His story serves as a cautionary tale against replacing divine blessings with fleeting pleasures, urging us to seek true joy in God's plan for our lives. Jesus' promise of transforming sorrow into joy reassures us of God's redemptive power, offering hope and renewal even in our darkest moments.

Questions for self-reflection:

1. Reflect on King Solomon's tragic journey from wisdom to waywardness. How did his pursuit of earthly desires lead to spiritual emptiness? Are there areas in your own life where you have experienced a similar struggle between worldly pursuits and spiritual fulfilment?

2. Consider King Solomon's introspection in (Ecclesiastes 2:2-11). How does his lamentation over the vanity of earthly endeavours resonate with your own experiences? Have you ever felt disillusioned by pursuing material possessions or worldly pleasures?

3. Ponder our Lord Jesus's promise of transforming sorrow into joy in John 16:19-22. How does this passage offer reassurance and hope in times of sorrow and despair? Reflect on a time when God transformed your sorrow into joy.

4. Reflect on the dangers of replacing divine blessings with transient satisfactions. In what ways are you tempted to seek fulfilment outside of God's plan for your life? How can you guard against these temptations and remain rooted in God's truth and purpose?

5. Consider this thought: "Christianity is not about acquiring joy through practical steps but about surrendering to the Holy Spirit's work within us." How does this perspective challenge your understanding of joy and spiritual growth? How can you cultivate a deeper reliance on the Holy Spirit in your journey towards true joy?

6. Reflect on the importance of submitting to God's will in experiencing true joy. In what areas of your life do you struggle to submit to God's plan? How can you actively submit your desires and ambitions to God, allowing His joy to permeate every aspect of your being?

7. Explore the role of prayer, Scripture, and service in opening ourselves up to receive God's joy. How do these spiritual disciplines help us align our hearts with God's will and experience His abundant joy? How can you incorporate these practices more intentionally into your daily life?

8. Meditate on the idea of God's joy becoming our strength. How does the presence of God's joy in your life empower you to face life's challenges with courage and faith? Take a moment to thank God for His abounding joy and ask Him to continue filling your heart with His presence.

Chapter 4

Rejoicing with Christ's Joy: The Call to True Joy

> It is our duty and privilege to rejoice in God and to rejoice in him always, at all times, in all conditions. There is enough in God to furnish us with matter of joy in the worst circumstance on earth. Rejoice in the Lord always, and again I say, Rejoice. If good men have not a continual feast, it is their own fault. Matthew Henry

Old and precious childhood memories

While searching for a hymn on joy, I stumbled upon an old one titled "Rejoice, my soul, and sing of your beloved Groom who gave you freedom and redeemed you on the Cross." This hymn, given to us by the late Rev Father Youssef Asaad, we used to sing gladly in the early years of our life at Sunday school and spiritual meetings at church, evokes memories of my father, a distinguished high school principal and eloquent English literature teacher. He was a man of great faith, education, diplomacy and success in his field, and widely respected in our community. Upon meeting me, people would frequently ask, "Are you the son of Mr so and so?" Hearing these words always filled me with happiness and pride, as the warmth, respect, and admiration associated with my father and family name.

Returning to the hymn, "Rejoice, my soul and glorify the name of Jesus. Wipe away every tear and sing the great song, looking towards heaven," prompts reflection on my pride in bearing the name of Christ as I once did in my earthly father's name. Do I carry the same pride as I walk the streets clad in my black priestly garments, bearing the Cross? Am I truly content with God in my life, secure in the knowledge of belonging to Him? Let us ponder whether we rejoice in our beloved Groom, Jesus Christ, and genuinely perceive Him as such.

A lesson in God's surprising Humour and unexpected calling

God has a way of revealing His humour to us. Allow me to share a captivating and humorous story from my life that left a lasting impact on my perspective.

During the early years of my priesthood, I was still adjusting to wearing my black priesthood garments. It was during a short holiday break in the city of Wollongong when a memorable incident occurred, leaving me with a valuable lesson etched in my heart.

Rejoicing with Christ's Joy: The Call to True Joy

My wife and I were strolling hand in hand through a city street lined with busy restaurants, trying to decide where we should dine. We passed a pub where a lively group of young people were enjoying their evening, filled with laughter and drinks. You know the scene: standing about in the open air, loud music playing, and perhaps some of them had indulged a bit too much, heightening their merry mood. However, as soon as they spotted us walking by, their cheery expressions turned to mockery. They pointed their fingers at us, laughed at us, and called out sarcastic comments.

At that moment, a surge of anger rushed through me, and my face grew red with embarrassment. I let go of my wife's hand and continued walking, consumed by my own thoughts. It felt burdensome just then to be dressed in black, enduring the judgment and ridicule of others. I pondered what might have provoked their amusement – perhaps they believed priests should not have wives, given the Catholic background where celibacy is expected. The reasons were unclear, but I was smarting with hurt and anger.

Little did I know that God had a lesson in store for me that very hour, a lesson that would leave a lasting impact on my life. It is fascinating how God often interacts with us, His children, in such simple yet profound ways, as if we were His sole focus so that we feel as if the entire world revolves around us. This divine attention makes you feel incredibly special, honoured, and drawn in the fascination of it. Just moments after that distressing encounter, I noticed a beautiful blonde Australian lady on the other side of the road. She looked into my eyes and then, without hesitation, began crossing the road towards me.

Initially, I was sceptical, thinking she was approaching to mock or tease me. However, to my surprise, when she reached me, she reached out and gently held the cross that hung around my neck. She bowed down, kissed it, and then placed it upon her head, declaring her faith in the Lord Jesus Christ's power, His Cross, and His ability to heal her eyes. Then, with spontaneous humility, she requested, "Dear Father, please pray for me."

At that moment, the stark contrast between the ridicule from the first set of people and the respect from this woman who honoured God and the cross that I wore struck me forcefully. It felt as if God were speaking directly to my heart, addressing my anger and shame. He was reminding me of the significance and responsibility that came with carrying His name. I felt as if He were telling me, "You do not understand the honour and dignity I have bestowed upon you by calling you to be my servant, to carry my name, and to wear my cross representing me."

From that day forward, I felt a deeper sense of honour and joy in my calling. God had not abandoned me in my frustration; He acknowledged, He *understood* my feelings, and He saw the sincerity of my heart. Most importantly, I felt a new joy because God had reminded me that I was chosen to carry His delicate and profound message of reconciliation and service.

In that second encounter, I realised that my appearance as a priest, adorned with Christ's cross, was not a burden to be ashamed of. Rather, it was a divine calling to represent Him, to proclaim His name, even without uttering a single word. The incident served as a potent reminder that God's love and guidance are always present, even in the face of adversity.

And so, I continued my journey as a priest, filled with renewed joy and dedication and a deep sense of honour for carrying the cross of the Beloved. I embraced anew the honour bestowed upon me, knowing that I had been chosen to carry a service of love, forgiveness, and, most notably, a message of reconciliation to all those I encountered. From that day onward, I rejoiced, always mindful of God's constant presence and guidance in my life. That is a genuine, true joy!

The word joy has all but disappeared from our everyday vocabulary these days. One reason is that we have confused joy with fleeting happiness and have come to believe it is found in pleasure, security, and prosperity. In succumbing to this confusion, however, we have believed a lie that comes from Satan. The Apostle James did not say, "Count it all joy when you fall into an easy chair." He wrote: Why? Because it brings out godly attributes in us that help us get through the difficulties of life. He continues: *Knowing that the testing of your faith produces patience. But let patience have its perfect work, that you may be perfect and complete, lacking nothing* (James 1:2-4).

COUNT IT ALL JOY WHEN YOU FALL INTO VARIOUS TRIALS.

Our vulnerability lies in our insecurity as Christians

Christians constitute approximately one-third of the world's population. Imagine the impact if these billions of Christians radiated joy, potentially transforming the entire world into a joyful Christian community. Yet, we remain vulnerable and weak, and the cause lies in our insecurity as Christians. Often, we do not live as if Christ were dwelling within us; we fail to comprehend Him, honour Him, or recognise His value. Christ Himself likened the kingdom of heaven to a merchant seeking exquisite pearls, who, upon discovering one of immense worth, sold everything to possess that field in which it lay (Matthew 13:45-46).

Within each of us lies a precious and invaluable treasure whose true worth we may not grasp. It is akin to giving a child something exceptionally valuable only to find it casually discarded or overlooked, treated as trivial. Let us examine ourselves: Does my soul rejoice in my Christ, my Groom? This question holds immense significance, allowing me to assess what truly brings me joy. Have I experienced genuine joy, or am I merely reacting to external stimuli? This serves as a preliminary inquiry; deeper exploration awaits in forthcoming chapters. What, then, is this chapter's message?

Previously, we comprehended and consented to the following:

1. Internal joy will emanate from within us, influencing those in our vicinity.
2. Jesus is the ultimate fountain of true joy, accessible to us when we remain close to Him.

Rejoicing with Christ's Joy: The Call to True Joy

3. The Holy Spirit serves as the conduit through which this joy is conveyed to us.

"Now may the God of hope fill you with all joy and peace in believing, that you may abound in hope by the power of the Holy Spirit." Romans 15:13

How does this joy penetrate our hearts?

This journey commenced exceptionally long ago when we first entered the church and underwent baptism, experiencing a spiritual rebirth. The significance of the Holy Sacraments should not be undervalued or underestimated. They demand active participation; they are not mere rituals we observe and then leave behind as we exit the church. We must immerse ourselves in their spiritual reality, study them, be convinced and deeply believe in their importance, find joy in them and most importantly living them in our life continuously, breathing them and being part of our awareness and deep conscious.

Take the sacrament of Baptism, for instance. It signifies a fresh start truly a new birth as the Apostle Saint Paul wrote, (2 Corinthians 5:17). It is a moment of joy as something radically new is formed within us. The old self or what Scripture calls the "old man," burdened with sin, is set aside, to be replaced by a new Christ-infused new creation, the new human being anointed

※

"Therefore, if anyone is in Christ, he is a new creation; old things have passed away; behold, all things have become new" with the Holy Spirit through the anointing with The Holy Myron (Gr. perfume; fragrant oil). Chrism is the oil with the highest level of sanctification in the Christian Church in which the grace of the Holy Spirit is poured out for the sanctifying and consecration to God of one on whom it is conferred. The symbolic 36 signs of the Cross that we receive in the sacrament of Chrismation, are a beautiful part of the rite of baptism, when we take the baptised person in a procession following the completion of the sacrament. It is like a dance symbolising the joy of joining a new member into the body of Christ, the church.

From this point forward, the Holy Spirit assumes responsibility for bestowing upon us this joy and cultivating His fruits within us. Every sacrament of the Church brings joy. The Eucharist in particular, is a source of immense joy, filling our hearts with gladness. As we partake in the Holy Communion, receiving the Body and Blood of our Lord and Saviour Jesus Christ, we are united with Him, and our hearts overflow with joy, and our tongues sing with rejoicing. "*He who eats My flesh and drinks My blood abides in Me, and I in him*" (John 6:56).

The oil used in the Unction of the Sick brings joy. Healing itself is a source of joy. Praying for all things and reciting numerous litanies also brings joy, as does offering prayers of repentance. The sacrament of the Priesthood is a cause for joy. Each member of the priesthood finds joy in serving the Groom's Bride, which is the Church, and the entire Church rejoices in this union. The ordination of a new deacon is a joyous occasion, as is marriage with all its joyful celebrations.

Repentance and confession are also sources of enormous joy—we have assigned the last chapter of this book to a consideration of this particularly important sacrament. When the priest places the cross on the head of the individual seeking absolution and declares during confession, "Loose every bond of our sins," this too is a cause of joy for us. The arrival of the priest in one's home brings joy, as does the entrance of a Bishop into a church, especially when accompanied by joyful hymns like "Epouro." Participating in Tasbeha, or midnight praise, is a joyful experience. When we rise early and venture into the cold to recite the Psali Watos, "Remembering Your holy name brings joy to our souls, O My Lord Jesus Christ," we are filled with joy. Upon completion, there is a sense of profound joy and happiness. Engaging in such spiritual practices allows us to experience the joy of participating in the Holy Liturgy, and then to proceed with our daily tasks filled with joy and contentment.

Living daily and hourly with Christ brings joy, as Saint Paul expressed, "*As sorrowful, yet always rejoicing*" (2 Corinthians 6:10). Engaging with the sacraments is a source of joy; therefore, meditate on them and immerse yourself in what they teach you. Just as you savour delicious food by chewing it slowly, relish the experience of praying the holy Liturgy in quiet contemplation. Delve deeply into its meaning and refrain from criticising its performance by others, allowing it to uplift you rather than burden you. The life of the Church itself is a joyous journey. Should

SINGING THE GLORIFICATIONS FOR THE SAINTS, PARTICULARLY FOR SAINT MARY, FILLS THE HEART WITH JOY.

you find yourself lacking in joy, return to the foundation – to the Church and her Sacraments. Our true treasure lies within these sacred rites. Take a moment to ask yourself: Are you living on the surface of things, or do you live from the depths both internally and externally? Consider the preoccupations of your heart.

Ask yourself: how joyful am I?

Am I a joyful Christian? Am I proud of my relationship with Jesus? Concern arises for the new generation who may have lost their sense of pride in being Christians or their identity, who resort to criticism of the Church and her clergy, exposing perceived weaknesses.

Let us examine ourselves and do not let anyone or anything rob us of our joy or our crown. The days of our life go amazingly fast. Be joyful with our Lord Jesus and say to Him, *"Fill our hearts with joy and gladness,"* as we recite in the Liturgy according to Saint Basil. May our God fill our lives and our hearts with joy, internal joy, not materialistic, worldly pleasure, but the joy that Jesus said not to let anyone take away.

Final words

In this chapter, we delved into the concept of joy as a profound aspect of the Christian faith. Drawing from subjective experiences and from the teachings of Scripture, this chapter has looked to the importance of finding true joy in Christ rather than in fleeting worldly pleasures. Reflect on the significance of bearing the name of Christ with pride. Delve into the distinction between joy and happiness. This chapter challenges us, through scriptural references and anecdotes, to rethink our understanding of joy and to prioritise our relationship with our Lord Jesus as the ultimate and only source of joy. The transformative power of the Holy Spirit and the sacraments of the Church in cultivating joy is highlighted. Readers are urged to immerse themselves fully in these spiritual practices. The chapter concludes with a call to introspection and a reminder not to allow anything or anyone to steal the joy that comes from belonging to Christ.

Questions for self-reflection:

1. Reflect on your understanding of joy as discussed in the chapter. How do you differentiate between joy and happiness in your own life? Do you find yourself seeking joy in temporary pleasures or in the enduring presence of Christ?

2. Consider our reflection on bearing the name of Christ with pride. Do you take pride in your identity as a Christian, and does this pride influence how you navigate your faith journey? Reflect on ways you can cultivate a deeper sense of pride in your relationship with Jesus.

3. Explore the scriptural references provided in the chapter, such as (James 1:2-4) and (Matthew 13:45-46). How do these passages shape your understanding of joy and its significance in the Christian life? Reflect on how trials and challenges contribute to cultivating godly attributes and deeper faith.

4. Reflect on the role of the Holy Spirit and the sacraments of the Church in fostering joy. How do baptism, the Eucharist, confession, and other sacraments contribute to your experience of joy in our Lord Christ? Consider ways you can deepen your engagement with these spiritual practices to cultivate greater joy in your life.

5. Take a moment to introspect on your current level of joy and contentment in life. Are there areas where you feel lacking in joy, or do you experience a deep sense of fulfilment in your relationship with Jesus? Reflect on

any obstacles or distractions that may be hindering your experience of joy in Christ.

6. Consider the author's call not to allow anything to steal the joy that comes from belonging to Christ. What are some familiar challenges or temptations that threaten your joy in Christ? Reflect on strategies to guard against these threats and cultivate a steadfast joy rooted in your faith.

7. Reflect on the prayer recited in the Liturgy according to Saint Basil: "Fill our hearts with joy and gladness." How does this prayer resonate with you, and how can you actively invite God to fill your life and heart with His abundant joy? Consider incorporating this prayer into your daily spiritual practice.

Chapter 5

What is the source of Joy

> *"And as soldiers think with joy about returning home, so also Christians constantly remember the end of their lives and the return to their Heavenly fatherland."*
>
> St Nicholas of Serbia

This world is the doorknob of eternity

The Rev Billy Graham was once asked a remarkably interesting question by an enthusiastic young American man. "I want to have the happiness Christianity promises, so why do I constantly feel defeated? Life is short, and I do not want to miss the excitement and happiness my parents promised and said is possible while living for Christ, but I have not experienced this at all."

You Shall Surely Rejoice

This is a question that keeps pondering in all our minds and hearts, especially today!

This is how the Reverend Billy Graham responded. "We must remember we are immortal and will live forever. To expect absolute, unqualified bliss in this life is expecting a bit too much. This life is only the dressing room for eternity. Jesus said that in this life there will be persecution, slander, libel, and deception. At which, He also said, *"Rejoice and be exceedingly glad, for great is your reward in heaven"* (Matthew 5:12).

Sadly, the word "joy" has all but disappeared from our ordinary Christian vocabulary. One reason is perhaps that we thought joy and happiness were found in this worldly comfort, ease, and luxury. The Apostle James did not say, "Count it all joy when you fall into an easy chair," but he said, (James 1:2). Difficulties and hardships for the Christian are what "growing pains" are to the growing child. No pain, no development; no development, no maturing; no struggle, no victory.

> ❋
> "COUNT IT ALL JOY WHEN YOU FALL INTO VARIOUS TRIALS"

The Gospel should never be dull, for it is the most exciting possible news we could ever receive. When we find it dull, it is a warning sign that something is going wrong inside us, and we need to take action to correct it.

Christians are to think and to act within the horizon of eternity. They should not be embittered when things do

What is the source of Joy

not turn out as planned. They know that *"the sufferings of this present world are not worthy to be compared with the glory that shall be revealed hereafter"* (Rom 8:18).

The key word in Graham's incredibly wise answer was the word "Eternity," when believers focus and get ready for eternity we will taste and live a joyful life. On the other hand, when Christians focus on the earthly short life, they will live an anxious life full of defeats that can steal and continuously rob our joy.

What you see determines your eternal perspective

Reflecting on my early childhood, I remember the frustration I felt in the classroom. Reading the writings of my teachers on the blackboard was a constant struggle. Day after day, I would go home, unable to grasp the lessons or complete my homework. The pressure was intense, especially as the son of a very distinguished school principal with remarkably high expectations from his children. It felt like an insurmountable challenge on top of many other ones.

Then, one day, my kind teacher back in school, Mrs. Stella, noticed my difficulty and struggle. After everyone had left for the lunch break, she asked me to stay behind. She had me sit at my usual desk and then asked "What do you see on the blackboard?" I squinted and strained, but I could not read much of anything.

That very afternoon, my father took me to the ophthalmologist, and so we discovered that I had myopia, which required corrective reading glasses. After that, my life in the classroom was entirely pleasant and enjoyable.

I share this story with you, dear reader, to illustrate a simple yet profound truth: sometimes we do not see joy because our spiritual eyes are out of focus and unable to perceive Christ clearly in our lives. Just as I needed prescription glasses to see the blackboard clearly,

WE NEED OUR SPIRITUAL INSIGHT MENDED SO THAT WE CAN RECOGNISE AND SEE CHRIST'S PRESENCE IN OUR DAILY INTERACTIONS AND EXPERIENCES.

Once the impaired vision of the eyes of our heart is corrected, the world around us—and the joy within it—becomes dramatically clearer and more vibrant.

In the book of Jeremiah, the Lord said to His prophet, *"Jeremiah, what do you see?"* (Jeremiah 1:11). We too might ask ourselves: what do our eyes see? The answer to this question is enormously important. It clarifies how we view our priorities in the world and how we live our short life on earth. Most importantly, by answering this question honestly, and taking remedial action, we calibrate our perspective so that it is focussed on earthly or eternal realities.

King David asked God in one of his Psalms, *"Oh, send out Your light and Your truth! Let them lead me; Let them bring me to Your holy hill, and to Your tabernacle. Then I will go to the altar of God, To God my exceeding joy, and on the harp, I will praise You, O God, my God"* (Psalm 43:3-4). David was seeing with his internal eye, the eye of his heart, when he prayed to *send Your light (Jesus) to Your holy hill (Your Church)*, to bring joy to me, and also when he had fallen into sin, and wrote his famous Psalm of repentance saying, *"Restore to me the joy of Your salvation"* (Psalm 51:12).

Salvation brings joy and happiness

Salvation, therefore, brings joy and happiness, and within the depths of Christianity, there is a wellspring of joy. King David also wrote, *"The king shall have joy in Your strength, O LORD; And in Your salvation how greatly shall he rejoice"* (Psalm 21:1). Holy Scripture is a message of joy and salvation and utmost hope; hence, we call it The Good News. When our Lord and Saviour Jesus Christ was born in the manger, the angel spoke to the shepherds, saying, *"For behold, I bring you good tidings of great joy"* (Luke 2:10).

When we concentrate on salvation, and the eyes of our hearts are looking to this great gift from God, we will be very joyful indeed. The light of our Lord Jesus and the joy of Jesus rejoices our heart and our life, *"Whom having not seen you love. Though now you do not see Him, yet believing, you rejoice with joy inexpressible and full of glory"* (1 Peter 1:8).

Before reading the Gospel during the Holy Liturgy, the serving priest puts incense in the censer and starts praying a litany – a prayer for the Holy Gospel, *"O Master, Lord Jesus Christ, many prophets and righteous men earnestly desired to see and have not seen and to hear and have not heard, but as for you, blessed are your eyes, for they see and your ears, for they hear."*

Blessed means how lucky and joyful to see these things, while all the prophets desired to see them too. That is why

King David said, *"Oh, send out Your light and Your truth! Let them lead me; let them bring me to Your holy hill and to Your tabernacle. Then I will go to the altar of God, to God my exceeding joy; and on the harp I will praise You, O God, my God"* (Psalm 43:3-4).

Let us see and focus on the joy of salvation! Isaiah the prophet saw salvation with his prophetic eye and talked of it many times, *"And in that day you will say: O LORD, I will praise You; Though You were angry with me, Your anger is turned away, and You comfort me. Behold, God is my salvation, I will trust and not be afraid; 'For YAH, the LORD, is my strength and song; He also has become my salvation. Therefore, with joy you will draw water, from the wells of salvation"* (Isaiah 12:1-3).

The water here refers to the Holy Spirit. The joy of salvation and spiritual good cheer cannot be expressed in words, but it can be felt in our hearts. Close your eyes and observe the Kingdom of God within you, enjoy the salvation, take pleasure in the reconciliation between God and ourselves. We were in enmity before but then were reconciled to the Father by our Lord Christ's death on the cross.

Enjoy the prayer of reconciliation when the priest, during the liturgy, takes off the "prosharine," a Greek word meaning "to offer an oblation," and refers to a cover placed over the holy elements on the altar, used after the Prayer of Thanksgiving, and removed after the prayer of Reconciliation (Spasmos). It refers to the stone that the angel had moved aside after the Lord's resurrection, symbolising reconciliation between heaven and earth. And then we are no longer enslaved, but we are made friends, as our Lord Christ said, *"No longer do I call you servants, for a servant does not know what his master is doing; but I have called you friends"* (John 15:15).

Salvation is when my eyes are focused on God and so my path is eased and lightened. Don't look back along your path at the earthly sweetness you tasted in the past, which but lasts a few seconds, such as something you bought to eat or to wear, or a joke or a song or any worldly pleasures, but rather focus only on your salvation, *"The Lord is my light and my salvation; whom shall I fear? The Lord is the strength of my life; of whom shall I be afraid?"* (Psalm 27:1); *"Therefore with joy you will draw water from the wells of salvation"* (Isaiah 12:3).

The great Prophet Isaiah continues, *"Praise the Lord, call upon His name; declare His deeds among the peoples, make mention that His name is exalted. Sing to the Lord, for He has done excellent things; this is known in all the earth. Cry out and shout, O inhabitant of Zion, for great is the Holy One of Israel in your midst!"* (Isaiah 12:4-6). He continues prophetically seeing the whole of salvation, *"For the Lord will comfort Zion ... Joy and gladness will be found in it ... Awake, awake, put on strength, O arm of the Lord! ... And they shall come to Zion with singing, With everlasting joy on their heads. They shall obtain joy and gladness, Sorrow and sighing shall flee away"* (Isaiah 51:3, 9, 11). Isaiah is talking about heaven and eternity. They enter the Altar and join their bridegroom in chanting. On their heads, there is eternal joy, no sadness or sorrow. We are not in debt, for our bridegroom, Jesus paid all our debt on the cross, and on our heads there is everlasting joy.

What is it, then, that makes us sad and anxious? What are we waiting and expecting from this perishable world? Are we waiting for a word of comfort from people? Are we waiting for something temporary and earthly to cheer us up? Are we waiting for perishable money to give us security? We have eternal joy on our heads! That is why David the Prophet said, *"The Lord is my strength and song, And He has become my salvation"* (Psalm 118:14). Wake up my soul and ask yourself, what do you see?

Looking into your heart, pray, "Restore to me the joy of your salvation"

Today, we are invited to look with the eyes of our hearts, to focus on salvation and joy. Not only joy but singing and chanting with joy, a joy that glorifies Him, that gives Him thanks for His salvation and redemption. We come across many beautiful, joyful promises, *"Your words were found, and I ate them, And Your word was to me the joy and rejoicing of my heart"* (Jeremiah 15:16).

THIS IS THE MOST PRECIOUS GIFT IN OUR LIFE, AND IT IS GIVEN TO US FREELY. WHEN WE READ THE SCRIPTURES AND UNDERSTAND THEM MORE FULLY,

My dear reader, the one thing that gives us the greatest joy is salvation. We are grieved when we lose it due to many factors, including falling into sins. When King David fell into sin, he repented with sackcloth and ashes and prayed, *"Restore to me the joy of Your salvation"* (Psalm 51:12). Do not live Christianity with external formalities, passing emotions and short-sighted worldly vision on the level of rituals and superficial meditations, but instead, enjoy into the joy that your Saviour has granted to you.

We are co-heirs with Christ; the Holy Spirit works inside us to infuse our hearts with the joy of salvation. Satan, on the other hand, constantly strives to rob us of this gift and to leave us wretchedly poor and naked, without joy and discontented. Hence, we go about the world carrying our spiritual failure, looking for stagnant puddles of water in cracked cisterns because the joy of salvation has died in us.

This powerful metaphor is used by God in His words to Jeremiah, His prophet, *"For My people have committed two evils: They have forsaken Me, the fountain of living waters, And hewn themselves cisterns—broken cisterns that can hold no water"* (Jeremiah 2:13).

- *Forsaken Me, the fountain of living waters*: God describes Himself as the source of life, refreshment, and sustenance, like a fountain of living waters. To forsake God is to abandon the true and abundant source of spiritual life and well-being.

- *Hewn themselves cisterns*: A cistern is a human-made reservoir for storing water. By making our own cisterns, we have turned to our own efforts and created substitutes for God's provision.

- *Broken cisterns that can hold no water*: These human-made cisterns are so defective they are unable to hold water, symbolising the futility and insufficiency of relying on anything or anyone other than God.

Let us then hold on to the call and the invitation extended by Saint Paul to his disciple Saint Timothy, *"Strive, and hold on to the eternal life to which you were called"* (1 Timothy 6: 12).

My beloved, let us look at the Cross, look at the hope, the faith, the love; wear the helmet of salvation, the hope that we have a place in heaven. Focus on it, close our eyes upon it, and talk continuously with our Lord about the joy of salvation, and say to Him, "Restore to me *the joy of your salvation"* (Psalm 51:12).

HOLD OUT FOR ETERNAL LIFE, FOCUS YOUR EYES ON SALVATION, DO NOT LET IT GO, DO NOT LET YOUR HEART BE OCCUPIED WITH ANYTHING ELSE!

Final words

In this chapter, we have attempted to explore the profound connection between joy and salvation, emphasising that the ultimate source of joy is found in our Lord Jesus Christ. Through Scriptural references and reflections on the writings of King David, Isaiah the prophet, and others, the chapter has underscored the transformative power of focusing on salvation and the joy it brings, the importance of seeing rightly with spiritual eyes, of internalising the message of salvation, and of cherishing the reconciliation between heaven and earth brought about by our Lord and Saviour Jesus Christ's sacrifice. Central to the chapter is the invitation to shift our focus from worldly distractions to the eternal promise of salvation, allowing the joy of Christ to permeate our hearts and lives.

Questions for self-reflection:

1. Reflect on your understanding of joy as rooted in salvation, as discussed in the chapter. How does focusing on the gift of salvation impact your perception of joy in your life? Do you find joy in temporary pleasures or the enduring hope of salvation?

2. Consider the passages and reflections in the writings of King David and Prophet Isaiah presented in the chapter. How do these passages deepen your appreciation for the joy that comes from salvation? Reflect on specific verses or images that resonate with you and evoke a sense of joy in your heart.

3. Explore the concept of seeing with spiritual eyes, as emphasized in the chapter. How does this spiritual vision enable us to perceive the joy of salvation more clearly? Reflect on ways you can cultivate spiritual discernment and deepen your understanding of the joy that comes from knowing Christ.

4. Reflect on the imagery of reconciliation between heaven and earth highlighted in the chapter. How does this imagery shape your understanding of salvation and its connection to joy? Consider moments in your life when you have experienced the profound joy of reconciliation with God and others.

5. Consider the invitation to focus on salvation as the ultimate source of joy. How do you prioritize the pursuit of eternal life and the hope of heaven in your daily life?

Reflect on any distractions or obstacles that may hinder your focus on salvation and joy and identify steps you can take to overcome them.

6. Reflect on the prayer of King David, *"Restore to me the joy of Your salvation"* (Psalm 51:12), as discussed in the chapter. How does this prayer resonate with your own experiences of spiritual renewal and restoration? Reflect on moments when you have felt the need to renew your joy in salvation and reconnect with the hope it brings.

7. Consider the admonition to hold onto the joy of salvation amidst life's challenges and distractions. How do you guard against allowing external circumstances or worldly concerns to diminish your joy in our Lord Christ? Reflect on strategies you can employ to maintain a steadfast focus on salvation and the eternal hope it provides.

May God rejoice our hearts and always give us the joy of the fullness and the joy of salvation.

Chapter 6

The Joy of Salvation

> "It was a moment of salvation, worthy of all bliss.... Thus He spoke the words of forgiveness, redemption, and everlasting life. He spoke the words of endowment and grace. On the Cross He did not condemn anybody, He did not punish a single person, despite all His afflictions: He did not come to destroy but to save the world."
> Pope Shenouda III

Saint Gregory, Wonderworker and Bishop of Neocaesarea

Saint Gregory was born in Neocaesarea of Pontus to parents who were not Christians. He studied in Athens, in Alexandria, in Beirut, and finally for five years in Caesarea of Palestine. Saint Gregory went to Alexandria, known at that time as a centre for Christian learning. Eager to acquire knowledge, Gregory attended the Alexandrian Catechetical

School, where the presbyter Origen taught. Origen was a famous teacher, possessing great strength of mind, profound knowledge and fervour of spirit. Gregory studied for eight years with Origen, who baptised him. Afterwards, the Saint wrote of his mentor: "This man received from God a sublime gift, to be an interpreter of the Word of God for people, to apprehend the Word of God, as God Himself did use it, and to explain it to people, insofar as they could understand it."

Then, in the year 240, he was sent as the founding bishop of his own city, wherein he found only seventeen Christians. By the time the Saint reposed about the year 265, only seventeen unbelievers were left there. The whole duration of his episcopacy was a time of continual, marvellous wonders worked by him. Because of this, he received the surname "Wonderworker;" even the enemies of the truth called him a second Moses.

Saint Gregory, the Wonderworker Bishop of Neocaesarea, manifested an ecclesiastical role more of a practical, pastoral nature, rather than of a speculative theologian. In his catecheses, he spoke the following beautiful words about joy,

"Rejoice before the Lord, because He comes." He is referring to the birth, the incarnation, and the Second Coming of our Lord Jesus Christ to this world. He adds:

> "Today, the ranks of angels rejoice with praises and the light of the presence of Christ shines brightly upon the faithful. Today, is a glad springtime for us, and Christ the Sun of Righteousness shines all around us with a bright light, illumining the minds of the faithful. Today, Adam is made new, and, having

soared to heaven on high, now takes a place in the choir of angels. Today, the whole earth is enveloped in joy since the descent of the Holy Spirit upon us has taken place. Today, God's grace, the hope of the unseen, shines through all the miracles which surpass our understanding, and reveals the mystery which was hidden from us before all ages. Today, the words of King David are fulfilled, *'Let the heavens rejoice, and let the earth be glad. The fields shall be joyful, and all the trees of the wood before the Lord, because He is coming."*

Our Lord Jesus Christ comes into the world, His light shining around us and bringing unparalleled joy to the entire world. He declares salvation to us – rejoice in the joy of salvation! This means living in reconciliation with our King, living a powerful life with Him. In other words, living a life of repentance and of peace with myself, peace with those around me and most importantly, peace with God.

WE CANNOT ENJOY SALVATION IF WE DO NOT ENJOY A VICTORIOUS LIFE IN AND WITH OUR LORD AND SAVIOUR, JESUS CHRIST..

When we are not reconciled to God, and have fallen under the yoke of sin, and are not living a life of repentance, we remain shackled by sorrow and grief. Saint Paul the Apostle said, *"For godly sorrow produces repentance leading to salvation, not to be regretted* (2 Corinthians 7:10). Our Lord Christ said, *"Most assuredly, I say to you that you will weep and lament, but the world will rejoice; and you will be sorrowful, but your sorrow will be turned into joy"* (John 16:20). The world will always rejoice in lusts and desires, we will grieve, but our sorrow will turn into joy, and the sorrow that we experience on earth, will turn into full joy in the Kingdom of heaven.

A life of conquest or defeat?

Let us delve deeper into the joy of salvation. On the one hand, we have before us a life of victory, and on the other hand, a life of defeat. The difference between them is that we either choose to live a life of repentance or a life of sin—itis that simple.

Imagine you have a strung bow with an arrow fixed in the middle; on the right is repentance and on the left is defeat and sin. What causes the arrow of my will to take sides? There are many causes. Grace and a life of holiness and prayers cause us to choose to live a life of repentance. Evil company, bad influences, selfishness, lack of spiritual insight and purpose in life and worldly desires make us live a life of defeat, conquered by our lusts and passions; it is our choice.

However, the key factor is the amount of love in our hearts. Our Lord Jesus spoke to us about the woman who entered the house of Simon the Pharisee, who washed Christ's feet with her tears and wiped them with her hair. Christ told her, *"Therefore I say to you, her sins, which are many, are forgiven, for she loved much"* (Luke 7:47).

When love fills the heart and overflows, care increases, anticipation increases, trust increases, and scrutiny increases, therefore, not only do we not tolerate sin, but we do not accept lapses into sin. When the love of the Lord

Jesus fills our hearts, the focus on the self. We become less selfish and do not focus on our own self-enjoyment; instead, we want to make the most of our life and journey with our Lord, obeying and submitting to Him. I always believe that the biggest defeat in our unrepentant life lies in accepting sin and accepting living a defeated life by Satan, dwelling there.

Sin means selfishness

Sin embodies a profound degree of selfishness. If we put a magnifying glass over sin and analyse it, we will find a lot of selfishness; the person who is sinning thinks only of themselves and does not think of the consequences of this sin for both us and the loved ones around us.

Every action has an equivalent reaction; everything we do must have a price to pay for and follow-up consequences. People who struggle with addictions not only destroy themselves but sadly destroy all those loved ones around them. Those who are unfaithful in their marriages or full of anger and dishonesty have no blessings and destroy themselves and those loved ones around them. All these things come at a hefty price tag. The devil feeds this selfishness through offering sensual attractions for us but hides the consequences of the price of sin, and sadly, we follow as being blinded.

There is always a contest between selfishness and the love of the Lord. The side that wins is the one that prevails. When someone asked our Lord, Jesus, *"Teacher, which is the great commandment in the law?"* Our Lord Jesus replied, saying, *"You shall love the Lord your God with all your heart, with all your soul, and with all your mind. This is the first and great commandment"* (Matthew 22:36-38). True love is the greatest medicine to help us overcome and abandon sin.

WHEN WE FIND THE LOVE OF OUR LORD INCREASING IN OUR LIVES, WE THEN FIND OUR TENDENCY TO SIN HAS DECREASED AND VICE VERSA.

Wisdom from Saint Anthony the Great

Saint Anthony the Great told his disciples, "The sweetness of God's love is sweeter than honeycomb. Believe in the Lord and love Him, and know, my beloved children, that all commandments are neither heavy nor tiring but true light and eternal joy for those who complete obedience. If one loves the Lord with all their heart, with genuineness and with all their strength, they will acquire the fear of God. This fear generates tears, and tears generate strength, and then, with the perfection of this soul, it bears fruit in all things."

So now, my beloved ones in the Lord, secure for yourself this power, the power of love we spoke earlier that everything has a hidden power, so that the demons fear you and the toil you practice is reduced, making you more spiritual, because the sweetness of God's love is sweeter than the honeycomb. This power directs us towards the love of God, and His love creates fear in us, and we will live a life of repentance and true joy in salvation.

The obstacles that we call spiritual diseases

In our spiritual journey, we often encounter various obstacles that can hinder our relationship with God and our growth in faith. These obstacles, which we can liken to spiritual sicknesses or diseases, trouble us in various forms, and challenge our ability to maintain a strong, loving, and committed walk with God. Addressing these issues requires us to recognise and confront them head-on, seeking God's grace and guidance. Below, we explore ten significant spiritual obstacles and insights on overcoming them through repentance, prayer, and a renewed commitment to our faith.

1. Diminishing love towards God—we must identify this and acknowledge it, saying we are sinners because truly we do not love God enough, or perhaps not with a genuine love, and then we must bring it before God. The angel of the Church of Ephesus said, *"Nevertheless I have this against you, that you have left your first love. Remember therefore from where you have fallen; repent and do the first works"* (Revelation 2:4).

2. Selfishness— is focussing on oneself while not caring about the consequences of one's actions, and this is fed by the devil. Consider the Parable of the Grain of Wheat; our Lord Christ said, *"Most assuredly, I say to you, unless a grain of wheat falls*

into the ground and dies, it remains alone; but if it dies, it produces much grain"* (John 12:24). Our ego must die with the nails of the cross, *"And those who are Christ's have crucified the flesh with its passions and desires"* (Galatians 5:24).

3. Bad habits— habits tie us down like an animal blindfolded, wrapped and tied to a waterwheel. This is what the devil does to us, he closes our eyes and wraps and envelops us day and night. We would like to be released from this yoke, but we cannot do it! We are hooked to a screen of pornography and cannot move, and we fall, and no one can help us up. There is no repentance, and the Holy Spirit has been quenched. The only way to solve this is to turn away and flee from it from it at the beginning before the evil thought invades us and sets in. Go to your confession father regularly and repent, continue to repeat the name of Jesus in prayer, or chant the following hymn to the name of our Lord Jesus Christ, "Give joy to our souls as we remember your Holy name. Take away from us all the causes of sin." This requires much struggle, but the grace of God will support you.

4. Forgetting the fear of God—this is what King David the Prophet fell into. Sometimes we are afraid in front of others but do not care that we are exposed before the Lord. Sometimes we care about our image and appearance in front of others, but we do not think that our Lord sees us, but He does see us and sees everything we do. So, it is particularly important to expose ourselves before our confession father,

to generate a holy fear, as David said in the Psalm, *"My flesh trembles for fear of You"* (Psalm 119:120).

5. Gambling against our eternity and our life—this is like a person who gambles everything and loses. We live and make mistakes unaware that our life may end at any moment. The Apostle Saint James tells us, *"What is your life? It is even a vapour that appears for a little time and then vanishes away"* (James 4:14). Sometimes we think that our Lord will send warnings, and sometimes we say that our Lord will not take us from this world unless we are ready, but this is not true. The Scriptures tell us to be ready and stay awake watchful like the wise virgins, *"Behold, the bridegroom is coming in the middle of the night"* (Matthew 25:6). The Scriptures urge us constantly to live a life of watchfulness, vigilance, and readiness.

6. Spiritual blindness—this often happens when we associate with the bad and corrupt company and when, as our Lord said, the blind lead the blind, and both alike will fall into a pit. There are those who lift us up, and there are those who make us fall. Beware of spiritual blindness. The only solution to this problem is to restore our spiritual understanding and vigilance and make our eyes focus on reading the word of God. In the Psalms, David said, *"Your word is a lamp to my feet, and a light to my path"* (Psalm 119:105).

7. Spiritual folly—our Lord Christ said, *"But God said to him, 'Fool! This night your soul will be required of you; then whose will those things be which you have provided?"* (Luke 12:20). Such a person does not

want to see or learn from their sin. Instead, they should be concerned to overcome and not repeat the same sin or be in the same place or sit with the same people. This reminds us of the profound words of a wise desert Father, Saint Shishoy:

"I do not remember that the devils tricked me into committing the same sin twice."

Perhaps the first sin was due to ignorance, negligence, weakness, a lack of knowledge of the tricks of the devils, or a lack of caution. After repentance and awakening, the scrutiny of our lives and guarding against sin must follow. Saint Shishoy's profound testimony resonates with the essence of true repentance and spiritual growth. His words encapsulate a pivotal truth: that the journey of faith involves a progression from ignorance and vulnerability to vigilance and discernment. Initially, our falls may stem from a myriad of factors—ignorance, negligence, or the subtle snares of the enemy. However, our perspective shifts as we walk the path of repentance and spiritual awakening. We become consciously aware of the adversary's strategies and the fragility of our resolve. With this heightened awareness comes a newfound diligence in guarding our hearts and lives against the recurrence of sin. Saint Shishoy's wisdom serves as a beacon, guiding us towards a life marked by discernment, accountability, and steadfastness in the face of temptation.

8. Deceptive appearances in worship—one may have external appearances in worship but lacks

spirituality from within. It is not right to serve inside the liturgy of the church and then to live a life of sin outside, to perform charitable deeds to be seen by others but to be spiritually empty within. This is like what termites do to a piece of wood. They enter the interior and are busy destroying it, but from the outside the piece of wood looks great! The solution is to expose our soul to our confession father. This requires honesty and humility because it is a complicated process like treating a disease.

9. Greed—King David was greedy for the wife of Uriah the Hittite. Greed is a serious matter, especially when it involves not only money and material possessions but also persons who belong to another. Thus, greed, not being satisfied with what one has, is not just for material possessions but can affect human relationships most destructively.

10. Stubbornness and rebellion—this problem often affects husbands and wives in their homes. A stubborn husband or a stubborn wife can destroy the home, *"For rebellion is as the sin of witchcraft, and stubbornness is as iniquity and idolatry. Because you have rejected the word of the Lord, He also has rejected you from being king"* (1 Samuel 15:23). The prophet Samuel spoke these words to King Saul because he rejected the words of the Lord. Rebellion and stubbornness can destroy the whole home; many often reject the advice of the bishops and priests, and therefore, the Lord rejects them. This is a difficult and incredibly challenging obstacle.

The pillars of all these diseases are pride, the ego and haughtiness, *"Pride goes before destruction and a haughty spirit before a fall"* (Proverbs 16:18). All these will grieve the Holy Spirit and quench joy, and lead us to defeat, and to losing the joy of salvation.

St. Amonas, a disciple of St. Anthony, said, "If the divine spirit left you and departed from you after you accepted it, seek it again, and it shall come to you."

If you once had a spiritual life and true love long ago, and then this departed from you, ask for it back.

When your heart is weighed down, do not despair. Set these things before you and keep them in your mind and thoughts, and thus, you will be re-ignited in God. When king David saw his heart full of heaviness, he said, *"When I remember these things, I pour out my soul within me"* (Psalm 42:4). He also had an amazing remedial recipe: *"I remember the days of old; I meditate on all Your works; I muse on the work of Your hands"* (Psalm 143:5). So therefore, remember the days of your first love. Weep and return to God and receive the sweetness of the Most Holy Spirit. Judge yourself and return to Him. The door is open. Joy and happiness are present, but we need to bring back our fiery spirit again.

THE SPIRITUAL FERVOUR WHICH GOD GIVES US IS LIKE FIRE. IT TURNS SPIRITUAL COLDNESS TO WARMTH AGAIN AND THEN TO A FIERY, BURNING SPIRITUAL LIFE.

Final words

Finally, chapter 6 delves into the transformative power of our Lord Jesus Christ's forgiveness, redemption, and everlasting life, which He offered freely on the Cross. Through poetic imagery and scriptural references, this chapter celebrates the joyous occasion of Christ's incarnation and Second Coming and the saving impact of His presence on earth. We underscore the importance of living a life of victory and repentance, grounded in reconciliation with God in Christ and love for God our Father. However, the chapter also explores the obstacles and diseases that hinder our spiritual growth and diminish the joy of salvation, such as diminishing love towards God, selfishness, evil habits, and spiritual blindness. Through the wisdom of saints like St. Anthony and St. Amonas, we are all encouraged to seek the renewal of their spiritual fervour and return to God's love, even in moments of despair or spiritual coldness.

Questions for self-reflection:

1. Reflect on the imagery and teachings presented in this chapter regarding the joy of salvation. How does the concept of salvation as a moment of forgiveness, redemption, and everlasting life resonate with you? Consider how our Lord Christ's presence brings light and joy to your life, illuminating the darkness and offering hope.

2. Explore the relationship between repentance and joy, as discussed in the chapter. How does living a life of victory and conquest, grounded in reconciliation with our Lord Christ, contribute to your experience of joy? Reflect on moments when repentance has brought about a profound sense of renewal and joy in your life.

3. Consider the obstacles and diseases outlined in the chapter that hinder our spiritual growth and diminish the joy of salvation. Reflect on any areas in your life where you may be struggling, such as diminishing love towards God, selfishness, or evil habits. How can you overcome these obstacles and cultivate a deeper sense of joy in your spiritual journey?

4. Reflect on the role of love in overcoming sin and selfishness, as emphasised in the chapter. How does genuine love for God and others transform our hearts and minds, leading to a life of repentance and true joy in salvation? Consider ways you can cultivate love in your relationships and deepen your commitment to Christ.

5. Explore the teachings of Saint Anthony and Saint Amonas regarding spiritual renewal and the return to God's love. Reflect on moments when you may have experienced spiritual coldness or despair in your journey. How can you seek the renewal of your spiritual fervour and return to God's love, even in challenging times?

6. Consider the importance of self-reflection and self-examination in the spiritual life, as highlighted in the chapter. How can you create space for introspection and contemplation in your daily routine? Reflect on the wisdom of saints and the power of returning to God with humility and sincerity.

7. Reflect on the closing exhortation of the chapter to live with purposeful joy and be a source of God's joy in the world. How can you cultivate a joyful and purposeful life rooted in the love of Christ? Consider ways you can share God's joy with others and be a light in the darkness of the world.

May our Lord fill our hearts so we can purposely live with joy and be a source of God's joy in the world.

Chapter 7

Joyful Service, the Heartbeat of Christian Ministry

> *"The way to true joy is through surrendering our will to God's Will."*
> Pope Shenouda III

To serve God willingly, the secret of a joyful life

Our teacher, Saint Paul the Apostle, gives us a wonderful outlook in 2 Corinthians 6:1-10, *"We then, as workers together with Him also plead with you not to receive the grace of God in vain. But in all things, we commend ourselves as ministers of God: as sorrowful, yet always rejoicing; as poor, yet making many rich; as having nothing, and yet possessing all things."*

Saint Paul is teaching us *"As sorrowful, yet always rejoicing."* These insightful words, almost unimaginably luminous, give us Paul's secret, which we make the core of this chapter!

Once upon a time, in the heart of Upper Egypt, I embarked on a service trip with the Shepherd and Mother of Light organisation that would forever change my perspective on life. It was the year 2016, and our mission was to bring hope and support to needy families living below the poverty line.

We were introduced to a family of eight during one visit to a small village. The weight of their struggles was palpable since the sole breadwinner, a man who works as a hard labourer in the building industry, a job that requires a lot of physical hard work and strength, was battling renal failure. He was struggling to provide for his loved ones. Financial resources were scarce, and the urgency for immediate medical assistance loomed over them like a dark cloud.

On that fateful day, I found myself feeling incredibly ill, struck down by a relentless flu. Weak and exhausted on a ridiculously hot sunny day in August, the hottest day of the year in upper Egypt, I longed for the comfort of my own bed. Little did I know that divine destiny had other plans for me.

Just as I was about to retreat to the car to rest and catch some sleep, a compassionate young lady approached, her eyes filled with concern. She pleaded and begged, "Father, can you spare a moment to visit and uplift this struggling soul?" Reluctantly, I agreed despite my weakened state. Together with another servant Moussa, we made our way to the family's humble abode.

Ascending the broken stairs, we entered a modest room below acceptable humane standards, filled with hardship and despair. The ailing man lay motionless on his bed, his body weakened by illness. Yet, as we stepped into his world, a glimmer of hope radiated from his eyes.

Undeterred by the circumstances, we began to sing a joyful hymn, its lyrics echoing the message, "Don't think that I have forgotten about you; do not think that I am far away. I bought you with my precious Blood and gifted you with new life. O my child, do not be anxious, do not be afraid. I am Jesus, the shepherd of the sheep."

The words carried a profound sense of faith and resilience. To our astonishment, the atmosphere transformed before our eyes.

In a matter of mere minutes, the room was filled with a chorus of voices, harmonising in unity. The power of chanting together and the shared experience of hope connected us all. It was as if the divine presence had stooped down and enveloped us, filling our hearts with an indescribable joy. As the song concluded, we opened the Bible and spoke of the reasons why worry should not consume us. In a twist of fate, my fellow servant and I collected all the money within our pockets, I still remember exactly the amount, a sum of 950 Egyptian pounds, all we had with us. It was the exact amount that the ailing man needed for his hospital treatment, a blood transfusion to control his worsening anaemia due to his renal failure.

Once shrouded in despair, the room was now overflowing with an astonishing joy. It was a moment of triumph, a testament to the miraculous workings of divine destiny and the unwavering faith of those present. The story of this extraordinary encounter spread like wildfire, igniting sparks of joy wherever it was shared.

From that day forward, this captivating tale of unyielding hope and the transformative power of singing that hymn resonated deeply within me. It served as a constant reminder that During the six-hour train trip that took us back to Cairo, we never stopped singing, "Do not think that I have forgotten about you, do not think that I am far away from you."

EVEN AMIDST THE DARKEST TIMES, JOY HAS THE EXTRAORDINARY ABILITY TO SEEP THROUGH THE CRACKS, ILLUMINATING OUR PATH AND UPLIFTING OUR SPIRITS.

And so, the legacy of that remarkable, unforgettable day lives on, inspiring others to believe in the incredible power of joy and reminding us all that even in the face of severe adversity, there is always a glimmer of light waiting to be discovered.

Our Lord Christ spoke very clearly in the Gospel according to Saint Matthew *"for I was hungry and you gave Me food; I was thirsty and you gave Me drink; I was a stranger and you took Me in; I was naked and you clothed Me; I was sick and you visited Me; I was in prison and you came to Me."* (Matthew 25:35-36). And when you serve Christ among the least of his brothers, you receive an abundance of joy and peace.

One of the secrets of joy and the key to a spiritual, joyful life is serving God. The service of our Lord and the works of love that we offer with goodwill, a contented soul, with sacrifice and a humble heart, lead to enormous joy.

A generator must burn fuel from the inside to produce energy and light. The wick of a candle must burn to give light to its surroundings. Likewise, with service, it opens the door for boundless joy.

Let us examine (Psalm 100:1-20), *"Make a joyful shout to the Lord, all you lands! Serve the Lord with gladness."* Whether we serve the Lord joyfully or serve Him out of necessity or obligation produces a different prospective outcome.

Reflecting on the joy of serving the Lord, I am reminded of my very first Sunday school teacher, Mr. Youssef Yacoub, who later became a very righteous priest, Father Sharobim Yacoub. He was a truly holy man of God, with a quiet and simple nature that radiated warmth. His ever-present smile and his joyful eyes behind his large glasses were his trademarks and a richness that always gathered us all in his heart.

Father Sharobim's joy was a living lesson, far more impactful than any words he spoke. His joy was evident in his actions—coming to all our homes, knocking on our doors, picking us up one by one, and walking with us as a large group, a big family, towards church while sharing stories from the Bible and Saints life till we arrive to church. His joyful face, voice, warm personality, and manner left an indelible mark on all of us, his children. We learned from his gladness and felt his joyful and warm love for the Lord in every interaction with him. His radiant spirit and dedicated service became a powerful example of how to serve the Lord with gladness, a lesson that continues to inspire me to this day.

This joy within a servant's heart is essential. It radiates positivity and is infectious. When we engage with joyful individuals in the Lord, their spirit uplifts us, inspiring a desire to pray and commune with God. Conversely, being amidst individuals who are constantly negative, filled with anger towards God, and always complaining about the service and clergy can dampen our enthusiasm for serving.

As sorrowful, yet always rejoicing

When discussing the joy found in service, we are reminded of the Apostle Saint Paul and his time in a Philippian prison cell. Arrested for confronting a fortune teller possessed by an unclean spirit, he intended to serve, sacrifice, and dedicate himself. However, he unexpectedly found himself imprisoned, chained to a wall with a log of wood for support, immobilised. Despite these circumstances, the profound power inherent in service brought him joy, as he wrote, *"Rejoice in the Lord always. Again I will say, rejoice!"* (Philippians 4:4). Why would Saint Paul repeat himself? He knew how hard such ever-joyfulness could often be.

Saint Paul derives this joy from his unwavering faith and commitment to the Lord Christ. In his letter to the Philippians, he elucidates on the source of his joy, explaining that his chains, though physically binding him, are in service to Christ. Despite being imprisoned, he perceives the divine purpose behind his circumstances, recognising that his suffering has contributed to the advancement of the gospel. Through his perseverance and unwavering faith, Saint Paul not only finds solace in Christ, but also inspires others, including the palace guard and fellow believers, to boldly proclaim the word of God without fear.

How strange that a man in prison could tell a church to rejoice. But Saint Paul's attitude teaches us an important lesson: Our outward circumstances do not need to dictate our inner attitudes. Saint Paul was full of joy because he knew that no matter what happened to him, the Lord Jesus Christ was with him. Several times in this letter, Saint Paul urged the Philippians to be joyful, probably because they needed to hear this. It is easy to get discouraged about unpleasant circumstances or to take unimportant events too seriously. If you have not been joyful lately, let the Holy Spirit remind you that true joy is found in the Lord and in the promise of His second coming.

Indeed, Saint Paul's commitment to sharing the word of God and spreading the message of salvation was unwavering, even in the face of severe trials. His joyful acceptance of his chains and the suffering they entailed exemplifies his profound dedication to Christ and his mission. According to God's promise, the sacrifice made for Christ invariably tends to joy, underscoring the transformative power of faith and steadfast devotion to the Lord's will.

The essence of joyful service, profound connection to God

Indeed, the essence of joyful service lies in our cleaving inwardly to our Lord and Saviour, Jesus Christ and never letting go of our deep connection to Him. His sweetness surpasses all understanding, infusing our service with an unparalleled sense of fulfilment and purpose. Like Saint Paul, we must centre our thoughts and actions on Christ, recognising that our service is a privilege granted to us by Him. Despite the challenges and hardships we may meet, our focus should remain steadfastly on Christ, drawing strength from His presence and relying on His grace to sustain us through all circumstances. As Saint Paul beautifully expresses it, who empowers us to persevere and thrive in every situation.

OUR ABILITY TO NAVIGATE BOTH ABUNDANCE AND SCARCITY, JOY, AND SUFFERING, IS ROOTED IN OUR UNWAVERING FAITH IN CHRIST,

Indeed, when our unwavering focus on Christ fuels our service, everything else falls into place. There is no room for petty politics or divisions when our hearts are consumed with the desire to glorify God alone. Serving God with pure joy and genuine love, without seeking recognition or validation from others, unlocks the transformative power of Christ within us. As we selflessly serve others for the sake of Christ alone, His image becomes imprinted on our hearts, illuminating our lives with a radiant joy that shines forth to all those around us.

Let us love the Lord and express this love uncomplicatedly! *"But I fear, lest somehow, as the serpent deceived Eve by his craftiness, so your minds may be corrupted from the simplicity that is in Christ"* (2 Corinthians 11:3). Our goal is to offer love for Christ and in Christ. The more our life, our love, and our depth with Christ grow, the more our service will have an impact on others. Instead of merely giving information, we will impart a living example of the life we live with Christ, our faith, the depths we find in the Scriptures and the life of prayers, the struggle we live in our inner room. Others will see us as joyful servants, rich in Christ, and look on us as role models and then distance themselves from the world with all its temptations.

Many simple servants-believers were rich in Christ and profoundly affected others. *"As sorrowful, yet always rejoicing; as poor, yet making many rich; as having nothing, and yet possessing all things"* (2 Corinthians 6:10). Nowadays, we spend all the time of our service without impacting others. Using many sophisticated means, we invent many new worldly techniques of service.

The desert fathers and mothers devoted their lives to constant repentance, seeking unity with the Lord Christ through fervent prayer and meditation. After spending time in solitude, deepening their connection with God, they ventured into towns and villages to proclaim the Gospel, leading many souls to Christ. Returning to their solitary places, they replenished their spiritual strength through prayer, praise, meditation on the Psalms, and immersion in the Scriptures. Their lives were characterised by continual repentance and spiritually reaching forward, allowing them to become vessels of the Holy Spirit's power. We would do well to heed these timeless lessons and follow in their footsteps. The Spirit of God remains unchanged throughout time, and His timeless truths continue to guide and inspire us today, *"Jesus Christ is the same yesterday, today, and forever"* (Hebrews 13:8).

People want to see in us a joyful servant, a joyful image of Christ, a true icon of Christ who reflects His life, having authority and power given from God, living in the depth of service, with a power over souls that comes of love, with authority over serpents and scorpions. Sometimes, the service is tiring, but not from within. It is only an external, physical fatigue. The body is tired but joyful from within, and because it is a service that gives and spends, souls will be reborn in Christ *"Till we all come to the measure of the stature of the fullness of Christ"* (Ephesians 4:13); *"My little children, for whom I labour in birth again until Christ is formed in you"* (Galatians 4:19); *"Also that we may present every man perfect in Christ Jesus"* (Colossians 1:28); *"I have no greater joy than to hear that my children walk in truth"* (3 John 1:4). Where do we find this power? The late Father Bishoy Kamel once said, "The journey of service and its sanctification begins at the altar."

The best lesson I have been taught on service in my life!

Just as a plant grows, so faith and love increase, bringing about cooperative encounters, and making the service joyful, so that wandering sheep return to their barn, people have been lost return to God. One of the amazing lessons taught to us by the great Apostle Saint Paul comes from his deep conviction *"And I will very gladly spend and be spent for your souls; though the more abundantly I love you, the less I am loved."* (2 Corinthians 12:15). I invite you my dear reader and servants to stop before this beautiful and well lived experience of the great Saint Paul and think about your service commitment to the Lord and His flock!

I vividly remember one moment many years ago when I first embarked on my service journey. On that Sunday, I regrettably missed attending the Liturgy. Father Bishoy Yassa—a very esteemed and righteous Coptic father in Sydney halted me as I entered the church, surrounded by fellow servants and children. He questioned me, "What brings you here today, and for what purpose have you come?" I replied, "I have come to serve, father." His response was a stern rebuke, "To serve with what? Have you partaken in the Liturgy today? No? Are you then seeking to serve through your own strength and will?" His words left me speechless and humbled. Despite the embarrassment and disappointment I felt, I am forever grateful for the profound lesson father Bishoy administered me that day—a lesson that continues to resonate with me as I pen these lines. I expressed my gratitude to him, kissing his hands and feet, and I carry that invaluable lesson with me for the rest of my days.

As father Bishoy Yassa so profoundly taught me This message is one I wish to convey dearly to my beloved brethren, especially to those servants who may unintentionally neglect their spiritual responsibilities—be it in the Liturgy, in their personal repentance

OUR SERVICE FINDS ITS TRUE BEGINNING AT THE ALTAR, BOTH THE ALTAR OF THE CHURCH AND THE ALTAR OF THE INNER SELF.

and confession, or in nurturing their own spiritual growth.

I emphasise to them that true service is not merely about being occupied with numerous activities but rather about bearing fruits that endure. These fruits foster lasting transformation in the lives of those we serve. It is disheartening when our efforts yield only fleeting engagement, leaving people unchanged once they return home and resume their routines. When we find ourselves spiritually depleted, devoid of the inner nourishment that sustains us, we become susceptible to the dominance of our own egos. We grasp onto control, stubbornly cling to our own perspectives, and inevitably, conflicts arise. Pride takes root, hindering our ability to embrace others with humility and love.

Indeed, all the ailments that beset our service stem from this inner emptiness. Either Christ reigns within us, guiding our actions and attitudes, or we elevate ourselves above others, ensnared by our own self-importance. When Christ's love and humility dwell within us, we naturally radiate His presence, and others willingly yield to His transformative power.

Thus, I am reminded of the timeless wisdom imparted by Saint Paul: "*Rejoice in the Lord always; again I will say, rejoice*" (Philippians 4:4). This joy, deeply rooted in our communion with Christ, is the wellspring from which our service should flow. May we, as servants, be replenished from within, embodying this joyous spirit as we follow in the footsteps of our Lord and Saviour.

The crucible of suffering that Saint Paul endured during his time in prison deepened his humility and became a source of profound joy for all who encountered him.

My dear fellow servants, let us take a moment to introspect and reevaluate our lives, and particularly the note of joy in our service. Let us examine our worship through the lens of God's Word and the illuminating guidance of the Holy Spirit, seeking insight and renewal through the sacrament of confession. Let us prioritise reconnecting with our spiritual fathers for guidance and accountability, and let us dedicate quality time to commune with God in the solitude of our rooms, immersing ourselves in His Word and presence.

Final words

This chapter reflects on Saint Paul's imprisonment in Philippi, where despite his physical chains, he found joy in serving Christ and advancing the gospel. His unwavering faith and commitment to the mission of the Lord Jesus Christ exemplify the profound joy that comes from selfless service. The chapter also explores the importance of joy within a servant's heart, as it radiates positivity and inspires others to draw closer to God.

Furthermore, the chapter emphasises the essential connection between inner spiritual nourishment and effective service. It warns against the dangers of neglecting one's spiritual responsibilities and urges servants to prioritize communion with God, confession, and guidance from spiritual fathers.

Readers are encouraged to reevaluate their approach to service, ensuring that it is rooted in joy, humility, and a deep communion with Christ. It challenges servants to seek renewal and spiritual growth, recognising that true joy in service emanates from the transformative work of the Holy Spirit within them.

Questions for self-reflection:

1. Reflect on the concept of joyful service presented in this chapter. How does serving Christ with gladness, sacrifice, and humility contribute to your understanding of true joy in Christian ministry? Consider the moments in your own service where you have experienced profound joy and fulfilment.

2. Explore the connection between inner spiritual nourishment and effective service, as discussed in the chapter. How do neglecting our own spiritual responsibilities and focusing solely on external activities hinder our ability to serve effectively? Reflect on ways you can prioritise communion with God, confession, and guidance from spiritual mentors in your service.

3. Ponder the example of Saint Paul in Philippi, who found joy in serving Christ despite being physically imprisoned. Reflect on how his unwavering faith and commitment to Christ's mission may inspire you in your own service. How can you emulate Saint Paul's attitude of joy and dedication to Christ in your ministry?

4. Reflect on the importance of joy within a servant's heart, as highlighted in this chapter. How does cultivating joy within yourself enable you to inspire and uplift others in their faith journey? Consider ways to nurture joy in your heart and share it with those around you.

5. Beware of the dangers of pride and ego in service, as discussed in the chapter. How do pride and self-importance hinder our ability to serve with humility and love? Reflect on moments when you may have struggled with pride in your service and explore ways you can cultivate humility and selflessness in your ministry.

6. Consider the call to re-evaluate our approach to service and ensure it is rooted in joy, humility, and communion with Christ. How can you align your service more closely with these principles? Consider practical steps you might take to deepen your relationship with God and infuse your ministry with greater joy and purpose.

7. Examine the impact of joyful service on your own spiritual growth and the transformation of those you serve. Reflect on how serving with joy and humility has shaped your character and drawn you closer to Christ. How do you envision your service evolving as you set yourself to prioritise joy, humility, and communion with God?

May our gracious Lord grant each of us the profound joy that emanates from serving Him wholeheartedly, a joy that transcends circumstances and is infused by the transformative work of the Holy Spirit within us.

Chapter 8

Living in the Spirit: The Path to Joy through Love

> *"In truth, the Lord seeks neither virgins nor married women, and neither monks nor laypeople, but values a person's free intent, accepting it as the deed itself. He grants to everyone his free will and the grace of the Holy Spirit, which operates in an individual and directs the life of all who yearn to be saved."* Saint Macarius The Great.

God teaches the Great Saint Macarius a timeless lesson

During one of his fervent prayers, Saint Macarius the Great was graced with a divine message which informed him that he had not yet reached the pinnacle of virtue attained by two women residing in the city of Alexandria. Filled with humility and a burning desire to learn from these paragons of virtue as revealed to him by God, the saint set out from the solitude of the desert of Scetis, now called Wadi El Natrun, best known today because its ancient monasteries remain in use, unlike Nitria and Kellia which have only archaeological remains. The desertified valley around Scetis may be called the Desert of Scetis. So, Saint Macarius set out in search of the humble abode of these women.

Upon arriving at their dwelling, the women greeted Saint Macarius with warmth and hospitality, who received him with open arms and hearts brimming with joy. With utmost sincerity, he expressed his earnest intention to glean from their wisdom and virtue, urging them to share their charitable deeds without reservation. Initially taken aback by Saint Macarius' request, the women humbly insisted that they were simple individuals living ordinary lives with their husbands, devoid of any remarkable virtues. However, Saint Macarius persisted, his persistent determination prompting the women to reveal the extraordinary depth of their commitment to righteousness.

With heartfelt honesty, the women recounted their remarkable journey of marital harmony and spiritual dedication. Married to two brothers, they had resided together under the same roof for fifteen years, yet not a single word of ill will or shame had ever crossed their lips. Their home was devoid of quarrels or discord, a testament to their unwavering commitment to peace and unity.

Despite their longing to embrace a life of monasticism, their husbands had not granted permission. Undeterred, the women had solemnly vowed to maintain silence on worldly matters until their final breath, a pledge that embodied their fervent devotion to God and their unwavering pursuit of spiritual perfection. They treated the entire household with equal love, sharing everything without any hint of favouritism towards their own children.

Moved by the profound simplicity and steadfast devotion of these women, Saint Macarius departed from their presence enriched and inspired. Their humble abode had become a sanctuary of holiness, wherein the virtues of love, harmony, and selflessness flourished amidst the ordinariness of daily life. And in the exemplary lives of these women, Saint Macarius discovered a timeless lesson: that Saint Macarius glorified God and said,

TRUE VIRTUE LIES NOT IN GRAND GESTURES OR LOFTY ASPIRATIONS BUT IN THE HUMBLE DEDICATION TO LIVING IN EVERY MOMENT A LIFE OF LOVE, INTEGRITY, AND FAITHFULNESS.

> "In truth, the Lord seeks neither virgins nor married women, and neither monks nor laypeople, but values a person's free intent, accepting it as the deed itself. He grants to everyone his free will and the grace of the Holy Spirit, which operates in an individual and directs the life of all who yearn to be saved."

The perpetual conflict between the flesh and the Spirit

In Saint Paul's Epistle to the Galatians, he speaks of the fruits of the Spirit, *"I say then: Walk in the Spirit, and you shall not fulfil the lust of the flesh. For the flesh lusts against the Spirit, and the Spirit against the flesh; and these are contrary to one another, so that you do not do the things that you wish"* (Galatians 5:16).

The perpetual conflict between the flesh and the spirit is a fundamental aspect of the human condition, and of the life of the believer. The spirit yearns for a higher, heavenly existence aligned with God's divine purpose and plan, while the flesh, originating from the earth, tethers us to earthly desires and pursuits. This inherent tension within us manifests as a constant struggle, often compelling us to act in ways contrary to our spiritual aspirations.

The spirit, imbued with the Spirit, the divine spark of life, seeks to transcend the limitations of the earthly realm and soar towards spiritual fulfilment. It aspires to live in accordance with heavenly principles, guided by the eternal truths of God's wisdom and love. However, the flesh, rooted in the material world, exerts a powerful pull, enticing us to indulge in the pleasures and distractions of earthly existence.

This internal conflict manifests in several ways, as the Spirit urges us to rise above worldly concerns and embrace spiritual growth. At the same time, the flesh tempts us to succumb to immediate gratification and sensual pleasures. Whether it be the pursuit of material wealth, the gratification of physical desires, or the pursuit of selfish ambitions, the flesh exerts its influence, often leading us astray from the path of righteousness.

Yet, despite the relentless tug-of-war between flesh and Spirit, we are not powerless in this struggle. we can gradually overcome the dominion of the flesh **and allow the Spirit to ascend to its rightful place of authority within us.**

The soul's journey is a quest for harmony and balance, wherein the Spirit triumphs over the flesh, guiding us towards spiritual enlightenment and communion with the divine. Though the conflict may persist, we find true liberation and fulfilment in God's eternal presence through our unwavering commitment to the pursuit of the Spirit's higher calling; *"But if you are led by the Spirit, you are not under the law"* (Galatians 5:18).

> ❋
>
> THROUGH STEADFAST DEVOTION TO SPIRITUAL PRACTICES, PRAYER, AND A DETERMINED CONSCIOUS EFFORT TO ALIGN OUR ACTIONS WITH THE WILL OF GOD,

The works of the flesh versus the works of the Spirit

What are the works of the flesh? What are the works of the Spirit? Saint Paul the Apostle spoke about the works of the flesh in Galatians, *"Now the works of the flesh are evident, which are: adultery, fornication, uncleanness, lewdness, idolatry, sorcery, hatred, contentions, jealousies, outbursts of wrath, selfish ambitions, dissensions, heresies, envy, murders, drunkenness, revelries, and the like; of which I tell you beforehand, just as I also told you in time past, that those who practice such things will not inherit the kingdom of God"* (Galatians 5:19-21).

The works of the flesh, as delineated by Saint Paul in his Epistle to the Galatians, encompass a range of behaviours and attitudes contrary to the principles of righteousness and spiritual well-being. These include:

1. Adultery: Engaging in sexual relations with one who is not our spouse.
2. Fornication: Promiscuity, all unlawful sexual behaviour.
3. Uncleanness: Moral impurity or defilement.
4. Lewdness: Indecent, suggestive, or lascivious behaviour.
5. Idolatry: Worship of substitute gods of our own invention, devotion to material or mental objects apart from God.
6. Sorcery: Practicing magic, witchcraft, or analogous forms of demonic manipulation of events or persons.
7. Hatred: Deep-seated animosity or hostility towards others.
8. Contentions: Persistent arguments or conflicts.
9. Jealousies: Envious feelings towards others' possessions or achievements.
10. Outbursts of wrath: Unbridled anger or rage.
11. Selfish ambitions: Pursuit of personal gain at the expense of others.
12. Dissensions: Factions, divisions or disagreements within a group.

13. Heresies: Holding beliefs contrary to Christian Orthodox doctrine.
14. Envy: Resentment towards others' success or blessings.
15. Murders: Taking the life of another person.
16. Drunkenness: Excessive consumption of alcohol leading to the loss of mind and self-possession.
17. Revelries: Wild and dissolute behaviour, often associated with excessive drinking or partying.

He then spoke of the works of the Spirit, *"But the fruit of the Spirit is love, joy, peace, long-suffering, kindness, goodness, faithfulness, gentleness, self-control. Against such there is no law. And those who are Christ's have crucified the flesh with its passions and desires. If we live in the Spirit, let us also walk in the Spirit. Let us not become conceited, provoking one another, envying one another"* (Galatians 5:22-26).

In contrast, the works of the Spirit reflect virtues and qualities inspired by the presence and guidance of the Holy Spirit within individuals. These fruits of the Spirit, as outlined by Saint Paul in the same passage, include:

1. Love: Selfless, unconditional affection and goodwill towards others.
2. Joy: Deep-seated happiness and contentment, independent of circumstances.
3. Peace: Inner tranquillity and harmony, even amid turmoil.
4. Longsuffering: Patience and endurance in the face of adversity or provocation.

5. Kindness: Compassionate and considerate behaviour towards others.//
6. Goodness: Moral excellence and integrity in thought, word, and deed.
7. Faithfulness: Loyalty, steadfastness, and reliability in commitments.
8. Gentleness: Humility, meekness, and a non-aggressive demeanour.
9. Self-control: Mastery over one's desires, impulses, and emotions.

Deeper insights into the fruit of Joy

These fruits of the Spirit are characterised by their divine origin and transformative power. They are the markers of spiritual maturity and inner transformation. As we cultivate a deeper relationship with God and allow the Holy Spirit to work within us, these virtues manifest in our lives, bearing witness to the transformative power of God's grace and love.

The Spirit leads the individual to live in the Spirit by crucifying the flesh with its passions and desires. The gifts of the Spirit can be found in (1 Corinthians 12).

Indeed, the sequence of the fruits of the Spirit outlined by Saint Paul, is itself a profound reflection of the divine wisdom inherent in Scripture. The progression from love to joy to peace holds a significant spiritual significance, illustrating the interconnectedness and transformative power of all the virtues in the life of believers.

Living in the Spirit: The Path to Joy through Love

At the outset of this sequence stands love, the foundational virtue from which all others spring forth. Love, as the pinnacle of Christian virtue, embodies the very essence of God's nature and character. It is the driving force behind all righteous deeds and the foundation of the entire Christian faith. When love permeates the heart, it becomes the catalyst of spiritual growth and transformation, inspiring acts of compassion, kindness, and selflessness towards others.

Following love is joy, the natural outpouring of a heart filled with love and gratitude towards God. It transcends mere happiness, which is often contingent on external circumstances, and instead emanates from the abiding, eternal source of hope and salvation found in Christ. As love blossoms within the heart, it gives rise to an abiding sense of joy that sustains believers through times of trial and tribulation.

JOY ARISES FROM A DEEP AWARENESS OF GOD'S PRESENCE AND A PROFOUND SENSE OF CONTENTMENT AND FULFILMENT IN HIS PROMISES.

Finally, peace crowns this sequence of virtues, serving as the culmination of love and joy in the life of the believer. In its truest form, peace is not merely the absence of conflict or turmoil but rather a profound sense of inner tranquillity and harmony that surpasses all understanding. It is the fruit of a heart submitted to God's will, trusting in His providence, and resting securely in His promises. As love and joy work together to cultivate a deep intimacy with God, peace becomes the natural outcome, anchoring believers in the unshakeable assurance of His presence and sovereignty.

These fruits' mysterious unfolding and arrangement underscores the divine order inherent in God's plan for our lives. Love is the fertile soil in which the seeds of joy and peace are planted, nurturing a flourishing spiritual garden that bears witness to the transformative power of God's love. As believers abide in love, they are filled with joy, and as joy abounds, they are enveloped in peace, creating a virtuous cycle of spiritual growth and renewal that reflects the very nature of God Himself.

Love stands as the principal gateway to joy, while hatred, borne of the flesh, plunges us into discontent and despair. The prevalence of depression and unhappiness among so many stems from harbouring the sins of unforgiveness, anger, and resentment. When such emotions take root, they quench the Spirit within us and drain away all our capacity for joy. To embark on a life of joy, we must first look steadily toward love. Love manifests in both earthly and heavenly realms, with heaven itself epitomising love in its purest form. Love is the very essence of heaven's language, currency, and code.

Failure to cultivate this love on earth renders the comprehension of heaven arduous, repugnant, and impossible. Consider the challenge of navigating a foreign country without understanding its language—the analogy underscores the difficulty of inhabiting a realm of love without first embracing it here on earth.

Love's three dimensions:
- Love God
- Love myself
- Love my neighbour

The three are particularly and equally important. In the Gospel of Saint Matthew 22:36-39, we read, "'Teacher, which is the great commandment in the law?' Jesus said to him, This is the first and great commandment. And the second is like it:

'YOU SHALL LOVE THE LORD YOUR GOD WITH ALL YOUR HEART, WITH ALL YOUR SOUL, AND WITH ALL YOUR MIND.'

To love God – to love God with all your heart, mind, soul, and capability. We can summarise the love of God into 7 points:

'YOU SHALL LOVE YOUR NEIGHBOUR AS YOURSELF.'"

1. Obey His commandment—s "But his delight is in the law of the Lord, and in His law he meditates day and night" (Psalm 1:2). Walk and obey in His commandment, "For God is my witness, whom I serve with my spirit in the gospel of His Son, that without ceasing I make mention of you always in my prayers" (Romans 1:9).

2. Be satisfied with the Lord—be satisfied with Christ and do not seek anything else. When we are satisfied

at work or at home, we do not want to change our situation, and we do not complain.

3. Glorify God *"You will show me the path of life; In Your presence is fullness of joy; At Your right hand are pleasures forevermore"* (Psalm 16:11); *"The Lord will guide you continually, and satisfy your soul in drought, and strengthen your bones. You shall be like a watered garden, and like a spring of water, whose waters do not fail"* (Isaiah 58:11).

4. Live for God—as Saint Paul said, *"For if we live, we live to the Lord; and if we die, we die to the Lord. Therefore, whether we live or die, we are the Lord's"* (Romans 14:8).

5. Bear witness to God—for you can witness to God, even without opening your mouth or speaking, but through your Christian conduct and behaviour with everyone around you, at home, at church and in society.

6. Persist with our Lord—be steadfast with your eyes focused always on the Lord. We are branches of the vine, steadfast in prayers, reading the Scriptures, partaking of the Holy Communion, regular in our repentance and confession, committed in our relationship with God.

7. Wait upon the Lord—either we go, or He will come, *"Wait on the Lord; Be of good courage, And He shall strengthen your heart; Wait, I say, on the Lord"* (Psalm 27:14); *"Amen. Even so, come, Lord Jesus!"* (Revelation 22: 20).

Final words

In this chapter, we have explored the ongoing battle between the flesh and the spirit that is the condition of our human lives here below, emphasising the importance of cultivating the fruits of the Spirit for spiritual growth and joy. Drawing from narratives and scriptural teachings, we reflect on the significance of love as the cornerstone of all spiritual development.

We began with the story of Saint Macarius, learning from the example of two humble women in the city who embodied profound love and dedication within their marriages and family life. Their lives teach us that true virtue lies in humble dedication to love and to integrity in our own Jerusalem – our home.

Next, we delved into the conflict between the flesh and the spirit, urging readers to align their actions with God's will to overcome earthly desires. By examining the works of the flesh and the fruits of the Spirit, we reflect on areas where we may be yielding to the flesh rather than walking in the Spirit.

The chapter then focused on the sequence of the fruits of the Spirit—love, joy, and peace—and their interconnectedness in fostering spiritual growth. Love emerges as the foundational virtue, catalysing joy, and peace in our lives.

Finally, we concluded with practical insights into living a life of love, emphasising obedience to God's commandments, satisfaction in Him alone, and faithful perseverance in our spiritual journey. By aligning our lives with these principles and cultivating intimacy with God, we can experience the fullness of joy that comes from walking in the Spirit and embracing divine love.

Living in the Spirit: The Path to Joy through Love

Questions for self-reflection:

1. Reflect on the narrative of Saint Macarius and the two humble women. How does their example challenge your understanding of virtue and righteousness? Consider how their commitment to love, harmony, and dedication to God's will inspire your own spiritual journey.

2. Think about the internal struggle between the flesh and the spirit in your own life. In what ways do you find yourself yielding to the desires of the flesh rather than walking in the Spirit? Reflect on practical steps you can take to align your actions more closely with God's will and overcome earthly desires and pursuits.

3. Consider Saint Paul's delineation of the works of the flesh and the fruits of the Spirit. Reflect on areas in your life where you may be manifesting the works of the flesh, such as selfish ambitions, envy, or outbursts of wrath. How can you cultivate the fruits of the Spirit, such as love, joy, and peace, to overcome these negative tendencies?

4. Reflect on the sequence of the fruits of the Spirit—love, joy, and peace—and their interconnectedness in fostering spiritual growth. How does love to serve as the foundational virtue from which all other fruits spring forth in your own life? Consider practical ways you can deepen your love for God, yourself, and others to experience true joy and inner peace.

5. Consider practical insights into living a life of love, such as obedience to God's commandments, satisfaction in Him

alone, and faithful perseverance in the spiritual journey. Reflect on areas where you may need to align your life more closely with these principles. What steps can you take to deepen your intimacy with God and embrace the transformative power of divine love in your life?

Chapter 9

A Glimpse of Eternal Joy in the Radiant Transfiguration

"The bright cloud signifies the glory of the Holy Spirit, which covers the saints as a tent." Origen

The Significance of Feasts in the Coptic Church

It is wonderful to learn about the major and minor feasts celebrated in our Coptic Orthodox church, each marking momentous events in the life and ministry of our Lord Jesus Christ. These feasts serve as reminders of the profound impact of our Lord Christ's life and teachings on humanity. They provide opportunities for reflection, gratitude, and celebration within the faith community.

The Major Feasts, focusing on pivotal moments in the story of salvation, underscore the core beliefs and doctrines of Christianity. They highlight key events such as the Annunciation, Nativity, Epiphany, Palm Sunday, Resurrection, Ascension, and Pentecost, each contributing to the unfolding narrative of redemption and grace.

On the other hand, the Minor Feasts offer a detailed exploration of specific episodes in the life of our Lord Jesus Christ, enriching the spiritual journey of believers. These feasts include Covenant Thursday, Thomas Sunday, the Transfiguration, the Escape of the Holy Family to Egypt, Circumcision of our Lord Jesus, the Wedding at Cana of Galilee, and the Entrance of our Lord into the Temple. Each minor feast provides insights into our Lord Christ's teachings, miracles, and interactions, offering valuable lessons and inspiration for us believers.

Together, the major and minor feasts form a comprehensive liturgical calendar that guides church's worshippers through the significant milestones of our Lord Jesus Christ's earthly ministry, from his miraculous birth to his triumphant ascension. These feasts not only commemorate historical events but also deepen the spiritual connection between believers and the divine, fostering a sense of unity, reverence, and devotion within the faith community.

The Transfiguration: Key Themes and Messages

During our Lord's Transfiguration, two personalities appeared with Him:

Moses, the esteemed Prophet who humbly received the tablets of the law and led the Israelites out of Egypt, embodies the principles of divine guidance and deliverance. His presence at the Transfiguration underscores the continuity between the Old and New Testaments, emphasizing the fulfilment of the law in Christ and the liberation from spiritual bondage.

Elijah the Tishbite, known for his fervent prayers and prophetic ministry, exemplifies the power of intercession and righteousness. His appearance alongside our Lord Jesus at the Transfiguration signifies the continuity of prophetic authority and the anticipation of the Messiah's coming. As mentioned in the Epistle of Saint James,

ELIJAH'S CONNECTION WITH OUR LORD UNDERSCORES THE IMPORTANCE OF PRAYER AND PROPHETIC WITNESS IN THE LIFE OF BELIEVERS.

"The effective, fervent prayer of a righteous man avails much." Elijah was a man with a nature like ours, and he prayed earnestly that it would not rain; and it did not rain on the land for three years and six months" (James 5:16-17).

The Disciples Witness the Transfiguration

Saint Peter, Saint John, and Saint James witnessed the Transfiguration of our Lord Jesus on the mountain, and it is from the writings of these disciples we take the Catholic Epistles, in which we read proclamations and much comfort.

Through the lens of Saint Mark's Gospel, we explore the awe-inspiring moment.

Saint Peter's response, though filled with reverence, also reveals human frailty and the struggle to comprehend the magnitude of what they are witnessing. His suggestion that they build tabernacles reflects a desire to honour the wonder of the moment, yet it also reveals a lack of understanding.

The overshadowing cloud and the voice from heaven further emphasize the divine nature of the event, affirming our Lord and Saviour Jesus Christ as the Beloved Son of God and urging the disciples to listen to Him. The sudden disappearance of the prophets Moses and Elijah leaving only our Lord Jesus with them, symbolizes His pre-eminence and centrality in the divine plan of salvation.

Through reflection and contemplation on this significant event, we are invited to deepen our understanding of our Lord Jesus's divinity, His coming as the fulfilment of the law and the prophets, and the importance of listening to His teachings.

The Glimpse of Glory Awaiting Believers

As we continue on the journey of this book, you will notice, my dear reader, that this is the longest chapter of all due to the importance and richness of Transfiguration and its vast importance for us.

As believers and followers of God, we need to trust and believe that tremendous glory awaits us, a heavenly reality that transcends human comprehension. It was promised, prayed, and requested for us by our Lord Jesus Christ. As we recite in the Litany of the reposed, "Eye has not seen, nor ear heard, nor have entered into the heart of man The things which God has prepared for those who love Him" (1 Corinthians 2:9).

This singular event on the holy mountain reveals the radiant splendour of our Lord Jesus, shining brighter than the sun, with His garments glistening like snow. In the presence of the prophets Moses and Elijah, representing the law and the prophets, our Lord Jesus is affirmed as the fulfilment of all the divine promises and the embodiment of God's redemptive plan.

Saint Peter's reaction, expressing a desire to build tabernacles for our Lord Jesus and the prophets Moses and Elijah, reflects the human struggle to fully grasp the significance of what they are witnessing. Yet the overshadowing cloud and the voice from heaven proclaiming our Lord Jesus as the beloved Son serve to bring home to them His divine authority and the necessity of listening to His teachings.

In contemplating the Transfiguration, we are reminded of our own ultimate destination—union with God in His eternal kingdom. It is a testament to the unfathomable depths of God's love and the boundless blessings He has prepared for His children.

THE GLORY REVEALED ON THE MOUNTAIN FORESHADOWS THE JOY AND FULFILMENT THAT AWAITS THOSE WHO REMAIN FAITHFUL AND WHO LOVE GOD.

Saint Paul offers profound insight in his Epistle to the Philippians, affirming that God will transform our humble bodies to be like His glorious body. He eloquently states, "Who will transform our lowly body that it may be conformed to His glorious body, according to the working by which He is able even to subdue all things to Himself" (Philippians 3:21).

This divine promise, even of a bodily transformation, finds its roots in the very dawn of creation, with Adam and Eve fashioned in the image of God Himself. Created from the dust of the earth, they dwelled in paradise, entrusted with dominion and authority over all creation. As it is written, "God said: 'Let Us make man in our image, according to Our likeness; let them have dominion over the fish of the sea, over the birds of the air, and over the cattle, over all the earth and over every creeping thing that creeps on the earth'" (Genesis 1:26).

Also, King David the prophet said in the Psalms, "What is man that You are mindful of him, For You have made him a little lower than the angels, And You have crowned him with glory and honour. You have made him to have dominion over the works of Your hands; You have put all things under his feet" (Psalm 8:4-6).

The Fall and the Redemption of Humanity

The Fall of Adam and Eve marked the beginning of humanity's struggle with sin and the consequences of sin, as succinctly stated by Saint Paul, "All have sinned and fallen short of the glory of God" (Romans 3:23). Yet, despite this fallen state, God's declaration that we are made in His image remains unchanged. We see echoes of this original divine imprint in the blessings bestowed upon Noah and his descendants as they emerged from the Ark. God's command to "Be fruitful and multiply and fill the earth" (Genesis 9:1), coupled with the decree that human being's life is sacred because he/she is made in the image of God (Genesis 9:6), reaffirms the enduring presence of this divine image within humanity.

> "But human beings, contemptuous of the better things and shrinking from their apprehension, sought rather what was closer to themselves—and what was closer to them was the body and its sensations. So, they turned their minds away from intelligible reality and began to consider themselves. And by considering themselves, preferring their own things to the contemplation of divine things. Spending their time in these things and being unwilling to turn away from the things close at hand, they imprisoned in bodily pleasures their soul which had become disordered and mixed up with all kinds of desires, which they wholly forgot the power from God in the beginning." – Saint Athanasius the Great

Though we are marred by sin, this image of God in us persists, albeit as a shadow of its true glory. Yet, there is hope for its full restoration. God, in His infinite mercy, devised a plan for humanity's redemption, a plan that finds its culmination in the coming of the second Adam—our Lord Jesus Christ, when at the end of the ages He entered human history in person. Saint Cyril the Great beautifully articulates this divine purpose, stating that "through

Christ's incarnation, humanity—ailing and corrupted by sin—was offered a pathway back to life and immortality."

Renewal and restoration of humanity

In Christ, the Life-Giver, humanity finds its renewal and restoration. Just as through Adam came death, so through Christ comes life and the promise of immortality. Thus, through the redemptive work of Christ, humanity is transformed from a state of corruption to one of incorruptibility, reclaiming its intended likeness to God. So, grace comes upon us, just as because of Adam we were cast to death, so in our Lord Christ, we are cast through death and take the form of immortality.

AS THE HEAD OF THE BODY, THE CHURCH, CHRIST LEADS HUMANITY INTO A NEW EXISTENCE, ONE MARKED BY GRACE AND THE TRIUMPH OVER DEATH.

Humanity's trajectory shifted dramatically with the incarnation of the Word, with the crucifixion, the sufferings, and the resurrection of our Lord Jesus Christ. In Christ, we find ourselves restored to the glory that once eluded us, as Saint John eloquently states, "And of His fullness we have all received" (John 1:16). The Psalmist David, in prophetic anticipation, speaks of the paths of life and the fullness of joy found in God's right hand (Psalm 16:11). However, despite these promises, humanity remained in a state of fallenness, unable to grasp the glory intended for us. Yet, in His boundless mercy, God exalted Christ and bestowed upon Him a name above all names (Philippians

2:9), positioning Him at His right hand, ready to restore to us the glory we had lost.

Ultimate Fulfilment in Christ's Glory

Christ, descending from heaven, assumed human form, taking the shape of a bondservant, and in that form liberated humanity from the shackles of death and corruption and ascended to the right hand of the Father, clothed in the fullness of glory. Redemption was thus accomplished, and the restoration process began—the restoration of the glory tarnished by the Fall.

As Saint Paul elucidates in his letter to the Romans, this restoration unfolds gradually. "Those whom God foreknew, He predestined to be conformed to the Image of His Son, that Christ might be the firstborn among many brothers and sisters. Those He predestined, He called; those He called, He justified; and those He justified, He glorified" (Romans 8:29-30). This divine plan, outlined by Saint Paul, underscores the ineradicably bond between Christ and humanity. "If God is for us, who can be against us? After all, God, in His unfathomable love, did not spare His own Son but delivered Him up for us all, ensuring that with Christ, He would freely give us all things" (Romans 8:31-32). Indeed, this chapter in Saint Paul's letter to the Romans resounds with the beauty of God's redemptive plan.

Let us delve into the profound truth encapsulated in the verse: "To be conformed to the image of His Son" (Romans 8:29). This implies a fundamental transformation within us, aligning our very being with the likeness of Christ. In his letter to the Hebrews, Saint Paul urges us, amid life's trials and temptations, to cast off every hindrance and sin that entangles us. Instead, we are to run with endurance the race set before us, keeping our gaze fixed on our Lord Jesus Christ, the author and finisher of our faith, who endured the cross for the joy set before Him, now seated at the right hand of God's throne, and eagerly awaiting our arrival (Hebrews 12:1-2).

Saint Paul further expounds on this transformative journey in his second letter to the Corinthians, likening it to gazing in a mirror reflecting the glory of the Lord. "But we all, with unveiled face, beholding as in a mirror the glory of the Lord, are being transformed into the same image from glory to glory, just as by the Spirit of the Lord" (2 Corinthians 3:18). This transformation, though initiated in the present, finds its ultimate fulfilment in the glory that is yet to come.

The Richness of God's Grace

We do indeed anticipate the dawn of a new creation, where those in Christ become a new creation altogether. The old order of things passes away, making room for the emergence of a new reality marked by incorruptibility, honour, and power (2 Corinthians 5:17). This vision of renewal extends beyond individual human transformation to encompass the entire cosmos as we eagerly await the fulfilment of God's promise—a new heavens and a new earth where righteousness reigns supreme (2 Peter 3:13).

This eschatological hope shapes our perspective, infusing our present reality with purpose and anticipation. As we journey towards this glorious inheritance, our hearts are filled with expectation, for we are assured that what awaits us far surpasses anything we can imagine.

A Glimpse of Eternal Joy in the Radiant Transfiguration

In essence, the Transfiguration serves as a foretaste of this future glory, a glimpse of the ultimate transformative power of God's redemptive plan. While we may not yet fully apprehend this glory, we live in hopeful anticipation of the day when we will be fully conformed to the image of Christ, basking in the radiance of His presence for all eternity.

> ❈
>
> IT EMBOLDENS US TO ENDURE LIFE'S TRIALS, KNOWING THAT THEY ARE BUT MOMENTARY AFFLICTIONS WHEN COMPARED TO THE ETERNAL WEIGHT OF GLORY AWAITING US (2 CORINTHIANS 4:17).

"I saw a new heaven and a new earth, for the first heaven and the first earth had passed away He will dwell with them, and they shall be His people. God Himself will be with them and be their God. And God will wipe away every tear from their eyes; there shall be no more death, nor sorrow, nor crying. There shall be no more pain, for the former things have passed away" (Revelation 21:1-4).

As things are, we do not as yet see this glory. That is why Saint Paul writes again and again, "For I consider that the sufferings of this present time are not worthy to be compared with the glory which shall be revealed in us" (Romans 8:18), and, "Because the creation itself also will be delivered from the bondage of corruption into the glorious liberty of the children of God" (Romans 8:21), and, "For our light affliction, which is but for a moment, is working for us a far more exceeding and eternal weight of glory" (2 Corinthians 4:17), and, "For our citizenship is in heaven, from which we also eagerly wait for the Saviour, the Lord Jesus Christ who will transform our lowly body that it may be conformed to His glorious body, according to the working by which He is able even to subdue all things to Himself" (Philippians 3:20-21).

His message to us is that we must forbear a while before we enter that glory. On Mount Tabor, at the Transfiguration, we can taste and experience the glory that is waiting for us.

In the Gospel, according to Saint Luke, we hear a profound promise: "Blessed are those servants whom the master, when he comes, will find watching. Assuredly, I say to you that he will gird himself and have them sit down to eat and will come and serve them" (Luke 12:37). Where and when will this glorious banquet take place? The Gospel of Saint Matthew offers insight, revealing that it will occur in the Kingdom, where "the righteous will shine forth as the sun in the kingdom of their Father" (Matthew 13:43).

Those deemed righteous, who faithfully abide by the commandments, who persevere with honesty through tribulations, sufferings, and afflictions, and die in Christ, will radiate with a brilliance akin to the sun. Just as on Mount Tabor, where Christ's face radiated the divine light, we too shall come to partake in His glory. Our humble bodies will undergo a transformation, being conformed to His glorious body—a testament to His power to subdue all things (Philippians 3:21).

The Apostle Saint John echoes this profound truth, affirming that while the full extent of our transformation has yet to be revealed, we have the assurance that we will be like Him when He is revealed. This hope purifies us, driving us to live lives of purity and righteousness (1 John 3:2-3).

Our destiny, therefore, is nothing short of remarkable. Those who overcome will be granted the privilege to sit with our Lord and Saviour Jesus Christ on His throne, just as He overcame and sat down with His Father on His throne (Revelation 3:21). In His final prayer on the eve of his Passion, recorded in the Gospel of Saint John, Christ expressed His desire that we be united with Him, would behold His glory, and experience the eternal love that existed between the Father and the Son before the foundation of the world (John 17:24).

In the heavenly realm, we will not become gods, but we will be united with Him in a profound and intimate manner, receiving new bodies and partaking in His divine glory. Reflecting on our journey—from the dust of creation to the heights of glory—we are reminded of the richness of God's grace and the transformative power of His redemption. This is why we celebrate the Feast of the Transfiguration, rejoicing in the unity of the Trinity and the promise of our exaltation above the world through prayer and devotion.

Lessons from Holy Mountains

The scene atop Mount Tabor unfolds a profound narrative of faith, where the disciples, represented as the struggling church, witness the radiant presence of Moses and Elijah, emblematic of the victorious church, united with us in the heavenly realms. Prior to this revelation, Saint Peter's human frailty momentarily clouded his understanding, prompting him to rebuke the Lord's destined path. Yet, in His divine wisdom, Christ unveiled the splendour of His transfiguration, imparting a profound lesson of grace and fortitude amidst trials.

Throughout Scripture, holy mountains serve as sacred ladders to the above, where humanity ascends to the divine, which descends to meet us. Mount Ararat cradled Noah's Ark, a symbol of salvation and renewal. Mount Carmel witnessed Elijah's triumph over the prophets of Baal, a testament to God's sovereignty. Mount Horeb, or Sinai, and the Mount of Temptation served as hallowed ground for Moses and for our Lord Jesus, where divine revelations and spiritual battles unfolded. The Mount of Beatitudes and the Mount of Feeding the Multitude displayed our Lord Christ's teachings and miracles, respectively, offering spiritual sustenance to the multitude. The Mount of Olives, where our Lord Jesus imparted His teachings to the disciples and suffered an agony of prayer to the Father, and Mount Golgotha, where He bore the weight of humanity's sins, attest to the transformative power of His love. On Mount Moriah and Zion, Abraham's sacrifice took place, and the earthly Temple was built to be sublated into the eternal Temple that was Christ's Body.

Yet, it was on the Mount of Transfiguration that the fullness of divine glory was unveiled, revealing the unity of the Trinity and the promise of Lord Christ's redemptive sacrifice.

In every ascent and descent, these sacred peaks resonate with the echoes of faith, guiding believers through trials and triumphs, teaching us to trust in the Lord's providence and grace.

My brethren, our Lord has given us many promises on earth and in heaven. Have faith and hope, looking to Jesus, the author and finisher

※

HAVE JOY EVERY DAY WITH JESUS, OUR LOVING LORD, OUR SAVIOUR.

of our faith, who, for joy, endured sufferings and looked for the cloud of witnesses.

The Promises of Joy and Glory

Let us conclude with Christ's profound priestly prayer from the Gospel of Saint John chapter 17, a testament to the boundless joy that fills our hearts through God's promises. In this final supplication, our Lord Jesus Christ, with eyes lifted to heaven, beseeches the Father, "Glorify Your Son, that Your Son also may glorify You." He acknowledges the authority bestowed upon Him to grant eternal life to those entrusted to Him by the Father.

As He proclaims, Eternal life is in knowing the only true God and Jesus Christ whom He sent. Our Lord Christ glorified the Father on earth, completing the divine work entrusted to Him. He revealed the Father's name to those chosen out of the world, and they received His words, understanding His divine origin.

In this prayer, our Lord Christ intercedes not for the world but for those given to Him by the Father. He petitions the Father for our unity, sanctification, and protection from the evil one, affirming their separation from the world but commissioning them for its redemption. He consecrates Himself for their sake, desiring that they may be one as He is with the Father.

Moreover, He extends His prayer beyond His immediate disciples, interceding for all who will believe in Him through their testimony, envisioning a unity that mirrors the divine unity of the Father and the Son. Through His sacrifice, our Lord Christ imparts the glory bestowed upon Him by the

Father to those who believe, enabling them to be united with the divine.

Ultimately, His fervent desire is for all whom the Father has given Him to be with Him, to behold His glory, and to share in the eternal love that has existed since before the foundation of the world. As He declares the Father's name and love to His followers, His profound wish is that the Father's love should come to dwell within them, uniting them in Him.

Let me share with you, dear reader, that the chapter on the Transfiguration filled my heart with immense joy and hope, sustaining my spirit with profound happiness throughout this book's journey. I pray that you, too, will experience the same uplifting joy and inspiration!

Final words

Chapter 9 delved into the profound significance of the Feast of the Transfiguration, exploring its themes, messages, and implications for believers. It highlights the event as a powerful affirmation of our Lord Jesus Christ's divine identity and purpose, offering insights into His relationship with the prophets Moses and Elijah. Through reflection on the disciples' reactions and the divine revelations on the mountain, readers are invited to deepen their understanding of Lord Jesus Christ's divinity, His role in fulfilling the law and the prophets, and the importance of listening to His teachings.

A Glimpse of Eternal Joy in the Radiant Transfiguration

Questions for Self-Reflection:

1. How does the Transfiguration conform to our Lord Jesus Christ's divine identity and purpose, and what significance does it hold for your faith journey?

2. Consider the presence of the Prophets Moses and Elijah at the Transfiguration. What do they represent, and how does their appearance contribute to the event's deeper meaning?

3. Reflect on Saint Peter's response to the Transfiguration. How does his reaction mirror common struggles in faith, and what lessons can be learned from it?

4. The overshadowing cloud and the voice from heaven affirm our Lord Jesus as the beloved Son of God. How does this divine proclamation resonate with you, and what implications does it have for your relationship with Christ?

5. The chapter discusses the transformation awaiting believers, aligning them with the likeness of our Lord Christ. How does this concept of transformation inspire and guide your spiritual journey?

6. Explore the parallels between the Transfiguration and the promise of future glory in the heavenly realm. How does this eschatological hope shape your perspective on life's challenges and joys?

7. Consider the significance of mountains in biblical narratives, including the Mount of Transfiguration. How

do these sacred peaks symbolize spiritual encounters and divine revelations in your understanding?

8. Reflect on the prayer from the Gospel of Saint John chapter 17. What insights does it offer into Jesus Christ's intercession for believers and the unity He desires among His followers?

9. How does the Feast of the Transfiguration resonate with you personally, and how might you incorporate its themes and lessons into your daily life and spiritual practices?

10. In what ways does the Transfiguration serve as a foretaste of the future glory promised to believers, and how does this anticipation shape your hope and faith?

Chapter 10

Rejoicing in Hope, The Anchor of the Soul

> "The soul that loves God has its rest in God and in God alone. In all the paths that men walk in in the world, they do not attain peace until they draw [near] to hope in God."
> Saint Isaac the Syrian

Till you draw near to hope in God

The above saying of Saint Isaac the Syrian and Saint Paul's "Rejoicing in hope" (Rom 12:12) distil for us the profound joy that comes from trusting in God's promises for the future. They are vibrant expressions of the faith that transcends present circumstances, anchoring its joy in the assurance of God's unchanging love and the anticipation of His future blessings and plan for us. This joy is not dependent on current situations but is rooted in the confident expectation of God's continued goodness and faithfulness. By rejoicing in hope, we celebrate the future with deep, unwavering gladness, knowing that God's plans for us are filled with grace and mercy.

The Cathedral of Hope and Faith

Chapter 12 of Saint Paul's Epistles to the Romans is known as the Cathedral of Faith. We gain much joy when we read this chapter, "I beseech you therefore, brethren, by the mercies of God, that you present your bodies a living sacrifice, holy, acceptable to God, which is your reasonable service. And do not be conformed to this world, but be transformed by the renewing of your mind, that you may prove what is that good and acceptable and perfect will of God."

For I say, through the grace given to me, to everyone who is among you, not to think of himself more highly than he ought to think, but to think soberly, as God has dealt to each one a measure of faith. For as we have many members in one body, but all the members do not have the same function, so we, being many, are one body in Christ, and individually members of one another. Having then gifts differing according to the grace that is given to us, let us use them: if prophecy, let us prophesy in proportion to our faith; or ministry, let us use it in our ministering; he who teaches, in teaching; he who exhorts, in exhortation; he who gives, with liberality; he who leads, with diligence; he who shows mercy, with cheerfulness. Let love be without hypocrisy. Abhor what is evil. Cling to what is good. Be kindly affectionate to one another with brotherly love, in honour giving preference to one another; not lagging in diligence, fervent in spirit, serving the Lord; rejoicing in hope, patient in tribulation, continuing steadfastly in prayer" (Romans 12:1-12).

Saint Paul states we are all one body. We have each our work according to the grace, gifts and talents given to us, and the plan God has for each one of us. He gives us guidelines for love and behaviour towards one another, he instructs our worship to be fervent and not lazy, rejoicing in hope, patient in tribulations and steadfast in prayer. In this chapter, we want to delve into rejoicing in hope. What is hope?? What is patience in tribulations, and what is steadfastness in prayer? And finally, why are these three placed together in Saint Paul's passage?

Firstly, what is hope? Why is it so important in our life?

Hope is one of the surest sources of joy, not only fostering joy in our lives but also sustaining it through turbulent situations. Therefore, we must constantly focus on hope and remain steadfast in it.

HOPE KEEPS US JOYFUL AND MAINTAINS A POSITIVE MINDSET WHILE NAVIGATING THE CHALLENGING AND NARROW LANEWAYS OF LIFE.

In the paradise of desert there is a remarkable story that is impregnated with profound hope in every detail and line. It is said that a brother lived in a monastery worshipping God and struggling to obey God in his destined new life as a monk. Due to the intensity of his struggle and inadequate experience of spiritual warfare, he fell many times into sin. Nevertheless, he persevered and endured, through the encouragement, support, and the guidance of his spiritual father, refusing to give up on the monastic life. He established a rule for himself and was diligent in observing it. In his prayers, he would say:

"O Lord, you see the intensity of my condition and the depth of my sorrow. Save me, O Lord, whether I desire it or not. For I am like clay, longing for and loving sin. But You, Almighty God, deliver me from this impurity. If You only show mercy to the saints, it is not surprising. And if You only save the pure, there is no need, for they deserve it. But as for me, the unworthy one, O Lord, behold the wonder of Your mercy, for I have surrendered myself to You."

He would say this every day, whether he sinned or not. One day, as he was engaged in this prayer, the devil grew weary of his unwavering hope and his admirable audacity. The devil appeared face to face with him while he was reciting his psalms and said to him, "Are you not ashamed to stand before God and utter His name with your impure mouth?"

The brother replied, "Do you not strike me with a rod, and I will strike you back with a rod? You lead me into sin while I implore the merciful God to have compassion on me. I will continue to fight against you in this struggle until death. I will never lose hope in my God, nor will I cease to prepare myself for Him. We shall see who will prevail you or the mercy of God?"

Upon hearing these words, the devil said, "From now on, I will no longer fight against you, lest I become the cause of crowns being placed upon your head through your hope in God." And from that day forward, the devil withdrew from him, for "he who endures to the end shall be saved" (Matthew 24:13).

Consider this for a moment: in the midst of the vastness of the desert and the long hours spent daily in his monastic cell, how did he find the strength to continue his journey and achieve victory? The answer is simple: hope. Hope has an incredible power to sustain us, keeping us afloat even in the most challenging circumstances.

The power of hope!

It is about trusting that God can mend what we have broken with our human flaws and our ignorance. Hope is indispensable for life; it is one of the essential pillars, along with love and faith. Together, these form the foundation of our

HOPE IS MORE THAN MERE OPTIMISM; IT IS A DEEP CONFIDENCE AND EXPECTATION THAT GOD, WHO ABOUNDS IN MERCY, IS AT WORK, READY TO PROVIDE, HEAL, AND RESTORE.

existence. It is impossible to live without hope. Love, faith, and hope are the three things required to live in this world. These are our capital investments.

Hope and faith, while closely related, serve distinct purposes in our spiritual journey. Hope pertains to our future aspirations and desires, providing us with a sense of optimism and anticipation. Faith, on the other hand, is our present conviction and trust, guiding our daily actions and beliefs. Faith is what we live with and believe in the here and now, whereas hope looks forward to what is yet to come. For example, I believe God has prepared a kingdom in heaven for us (faith), and I hope, through God's grace, to be in His kingdom one day (hope). Thus, faith anchors us in the present, while hope propels us toward the future.

After Adam was removed from paradise, finally, after thousands of years, humanity had hope, and lived with this hope due to the promises Saint Paul tells us in Hebrews. Hope is essential in our lives. If we lose hope, we will be defeated by the devil. It is for this reason Satan always tries to break our hope, especially after we have fallen into sin. Consider the monk who has been attacked by Satan; the monk says to him, "You strike me with a rod, and I strike you with a rod." He has continuous hope.

Our hope is in our eternal life. Saint Paul tells us this in his first epistle to the Corinthians, "If in this life only we have hope in Christ, we are of all men the most pitiable" (1 Corinthians 15:19). Hope in the return of a sinner who repents, just like the father of the Prodigal Son had hope in his son's return.

Hopeful till the end

My brethren, if you have a loved one who is far away from God, never lose hope. The Lord gave us an excellent example while He was on the Cross during His last moments on earth. He gave the thief on His right-side hope. The thief said to our Lord, "Remember me Lord when You come to Your Kingdom" (Luke 23:42). The Lord answered him, "Today you will be in Paradise with Me" (Luke 23:43).

Our Lord had a great hope in the return of Zacchaeus, the Tax Collector. Also, He walked a long way, over 6 hours, uphill, in the heat, to see the Samaritan Woman; He had great hope for her return. Our Lord did not lose hope in Jonah when he tried to escape from Him. The Gospel of

Saint Matthew tells us, "A bruised reed He will not break, and smoking flax He will not quench" (Matthew 12:20). There is still a flicker of hope even in a smoking flax.

Isaac's hope for Jacob's transformation

That we sustain our hope is crucial, especially in times of adversity or when facing challenges. Hope empowers us to persevere to continue praying and believing for change, even if we do not see immediate results. Sometimes, the change we hope for may not manifest in our lifetime, but our hope plants a seed that can eventually bear fruit, whether in our own lives or in the lives of others.

IT IS ABOUT BELIEVING IN THE POSSIBILITY OF HEALING, TRANSFORMATION, AND A BRIGHTER TOMORROW, EVEN WHEN THE PRESENT CIRCUMSTANCES SEEM BLEAK.

The story of Isaac and Jacob illustrates well the importance of perseverance and enduring hope, even to the hour of our death. Despite not witnessing Jacob's transformation during his lifetime, Isaac remained faithful and trusting in God's plan. Jacob's change did indeed come later, demonstrating that God works in His own timing and according to His own divine purposes.

The example of Isaac reminds us that even when we do not see immediate results or the fulfilment of our hopes, we must continue to trust in God and His promises. Hope should remain a steadfast anchor in our lives, sustaining us through trials and uncertainties. As believers, we draw strength from the assurance that all things are possible through Christ, who empowers us to endure and overcome every challenge we face.

Isaac did not live to see Jacob when he became Israel. Indeed, at the time of Isaac's death, Jacob was still a deceiver. The change in Jacob came later; all things are possible to the believer; "I can do all things through Christ who strengthens me" (Philippians 4:13). Hope should never disappear from our lives.

The Psalms, a wellspring of hope leading to joy

These ancient songs and prayers capture the depth of human emotion, from despair to elation, and consistently point us toward the steadfast love and faithfulness of God. By immersing ourselves in the Psalms, we tap into a wellspring of hope that strengthens our spirit and renews our trust in God's promises.

THE PSALMS ARE AN ENORMOUS FUND OF HOPE FOR US, OFFERING US PROFOUND ENCOURAGEMENT AND REASSURANCE THROUGHOUT LIFE'S CHALLENGES, YIELDING JOY.

The Psalms contain the most joy-giving hope. Praying with the Psalms shows us many of God's promises; "Wait on the Lord; Be of good courage, and He shall strengthen your heart; Wait, I say, on the Lord!" (Psalm 27:14). Every Psalm contains a key of hope. If you pray ten Psalms, you gain ten keys of hope, giving you strength and joy.

When God opens, no one shall shut!

Maintaining hope in God's sovereignty and providence is essential in our earthly journey. Even when we cannot comprehend how God works in our lives or understand His divine plans, we hold on to the assurance that He is always present to us and actively involved in our circumstances.

Having hope in God means trusting that He is aware of our problems and challenges, and that He is working behind the scenes for our good. It is about acknowledging His supreme authority and recognising that He is the ultimate ruler over all things, both in heaven and on earth. By entrusting our concerns to God and placing our hope in His unfailing love and wisdom, we can find peace and reassurance amidst life's uncertainties. Our hope in God's faithfulness sustains us through grim times and strengthens our resolve to persevere in faith, knowing that He is always working for our welfare and His glory. It is as God promised in the book of Joshua, "I will be with you. I will not leave you nor forsake you. Be strong and of good courage" (Joshua 1:5-6).

God is within us, "more intimate to us than we are to ourselves" as Saint Augustine says; He has great mercy, and He is always faithful and, as we said above, he knows his own time. Whatever we ask for, we have hope that we will get it. Having hope gives us internal joy. Do not try to find joy outside or in some other place than in him because that way, we will never obtain that true, holy joy that always

HAVE HOPE THAT WHEN GOD OPENS, NO ONE SHALL SHUT, AND HAVE HOPE THAT GOD HAS A TIME FOR EVERYTHING.

looks to God's promises. Joseph trusted in God, and had hope that his life would change, although nothing around him indicated this.

At times, when we experience tribulations, Satan's voice is disturbingly loud, trying to convince us that this problem is too complicated and will never be resolved. Whether it be something in ourselves, at home, at church, our service, our relationships, he tries to show us that there is no solution to this problem, and he makes many excuses for it not being solved. Satan always shifts the situation to hopelessness and impossibility, to expecting no solution. It is ever his way because he wants to drag us down to despair.

God, on the contrary, says to us again and again: "Do not be afraid." The Psalmist tells us, "I will lift up my eyes to the hills—From whence comes my help? My help comes from the Lord" (Psalm 121:1). Wait on the Lord and do not lose hope, "rejoicing in hope" (Romans 12:12), "Wait on the Lord; Be of good courage, And He shall strengthen your heart; Wait, I say, on the Lord" (Psalm 27:14), "But those who wait on the Lord Shall renew their strength, they shall mount up with wings like eagles, They shall run and not be weary, they shall walk and not faint" (Isaiah 40:31).

Always say to God, "Be it according to Your will, for You are My Father. You always choose the good for me, even when, at times, it is bitter. I believe and trust in You." Sometimes, we trust others more than God; we trust people's worldly solutions and their persuasive words, and we forget to stand before God, ask Him, and say, "My God, You are the Father of all hope."

As long as I live, I will hope

In Ecclesiastes, we read, "To all the living there is hope" (Ecclesiastes 9:4). Think of that: as long as I live, I will hope! For that is what it says, "to all the living there is hope" (Ecclesiastes 9:4).

I adore this verse of Scripture; I live by this verse! I heed its word by trusting for the morrow, for needed changes, for every problem that crops up, for our children, our life, and our church. They are all in God's hands (Ecclesiastes 9:1). God cups us all in His hands and protects us in His eyes and no one touches us unless it is with His permission. This word is a fountain of hope and joy in my life that never fails and will never fail to pump a continuous and steady flow of joy into my heart and soul. That verse from Ecclesiastes beautifully encapsulates the essence of hope and the enduring belief in tomorrow's possibilities. It serves as a beacon of encouragement and reassurance, reminding us that if there is life, there is hope. This profound truth grounds our faith and sustains us through life's uncertainties and challenges.

Living by this verse is a testament to our unwavering trust in God's providence and sovereignty. It reflects a deep-seated confidence in His ability to bring about change, resolution, and redemption in every aspect of our lives. In times of doubt or difficulty, this verse serves as a reminder to place our trust in God's unfailing love and faithfulness. Trusting for the morrow means entrusting our worries, fears, and aspirations into God's capable hands. It means acknowledging that He holds the future and that His plans for us are good and purposeful. With this assurance, we can face each day with renewed hope and confidence, knowing that God is with us every step of the way. Never doubt that God has always a plan!

Let the weak say, 'I am strong'

The book of Joel has a golden powerful verse that is often overlooked. It says, "Let the weak say, 'I am strong'" (Joel 3:10).

Do you know much about Gideon? Gideon, the underdog—the underestimated, the little guy, the disadvantaged—whom no one would think could achieve victory – except God! From weak to mighty, Gideon's story in Judges 6 exemplifies how God loves an underdog, and we all cherish stories where the unlikeliest hero triumphs. It is like when an unranked local football team upsets Liverpool FC or Manchester City, and the fans storm the field in jubilation. Gideon embodies the ultimate underdog, who is nonetheless chosen by God, for he often picks those whom the world overlooks so that His glory may shines through.

When the angel of the Lord approached Gideon, saying, "The Lord is with you, mighty man of valor!" (Judges 6:12), Israel was deep in disobedience, oppressed by the Midianites (Judges 6:1). The Midianites would raid and strip Israel of their harvest and livestock, leaving the nation in a crisis. "Israel was brought very low because of Midian. And the people of Israel cried out for help to the Lord" (Judges 6:6). The Lord then turned to Gideon, saying, "Go in this might of yours and save Israel from the hand of Midian; do not I send you?" Gideon responded, "Please, Lord, how can I save Israel? Behold, my clan is the weakest in Manasseh, and I am the least in my father's house" (Judges 6:14-15).

This story is so hopeful because Gideon, the least among the least clan, was hiding when approached by the angel of the Lord, and yet he called him "mighty man of valor" and instructed him to "Go in this might of yours." Gideon might have wondered if the angel meant someone else, but God sees potential where we see none. He speaks of the future as if it is already present because, of course, with God, it is! God knew that Gideon's tiny force of 300 farmers and shepherds could never defeat the 135,000 seasoned Midianite soldiers on their own, and yet with God, all things are possible (Matthew 19:26). Therefore, do not ever lose hope, even if the odds seem insurmountable. In the end, it was said of Gideon, "God has given into his hand Midian and all the camp" (Judges 7:14c). It was God's victory, not Gideon's, ensuring that all glory went to God.

As we continue to lean on this foundational truth, may we find peace in knowing that our lives, our families, our churches, and all that concerns us are securely held in God's hands. His protection surrounds us, His grace sustains us, and His love never fails.

The hope that comes from knowing that we are children of God surpasses any earthly wealth, power, or glamour. As His beloved children, we are richly blessed with the assurance of His love, provision, and guidance for our lives. This hope fills our hearts with a joy that transcends the fleeting pleasures of the world.

It is a hope that anchors our souls and sustains us through every season of life.

As heirs of God's kingdom, we are indeed incredibly rich. Our true wealth lies not in material possessions or worldly accolades but in the priceless gift of salvation and the eternal inheritance that awaits us in heaven. May we always treasure this hope that yields joy and rejoice in the abundance of blessings from being called children of the most High God.

> ❋
> IN GOD, WE FIND THE ULTIMATE SOURCE OF HOPE THAT YIELDS JOY —A HOPE THAT IS STEADFAST AND UNWAVERING, EVEN AMID LIFE'S TRIALS AND CHALLENGES.

Final words

This chapter delved into the promise of hope as a fundamental aspect of the Christian faith, drawing insights from Saint Paul's teachings and other examples in Scripture. Hope is portrayed as essential for navigating life's challenges, sustaining faith, and finding joy in God's promises. Through various biblical narratives and verses, this chapter has emphasized the transformative power of hope, urging readers to cultivate and maintain it even amidst trials and uncertainties.

Questions for self-reflection:

1. How do you personally define hope, and what role does it play in your life?

2. Reflect on a time when you felt hopeless. How did you overcome that feeling, and what role did your faith play in it?

3. Consider the importance of hope in relationships, both with God and with others. How does hope influence your interactions and attitudes towards others?

4. In what ways can you cultivate a more hopeful outlook in your daily life, especially during challenging times?

5. Think about a specific area of your life where you need to nurture hope. What steps can you take to strengthen your hope and trust in God's plan?

6. How does hope intersect with your understanding of love and faith? In what ways do these three virtues support and complement each other?

7. Reflect on the examples of hope provided in the chapter, such as the thief on the cross and the parable of the Prodigal Son. How do these stories inspire you to maintain hope in your own life?

These questions are designed to encourage introspection and spiritual growth, prompting readers to explore the significance of hope in their faith journey and daily experiences.

You Shall Surely Rejoice

May God rejoice in our hope in life. May he always increase our faith, hope, love, and richness in Him. May God fill our hearts with joy and happiness and rejoice in hope for the future.

Chapter 11

Rejoicing in Submission and Simplicity: Lessons from the Life of Saint Mary

> *"Hail, Mother of God and of us all, 'heaven' where God dwells, 'throne' from which our Lord dispenses all grace, 'fair daughter, Virgin, honour, glory and firmament of our Church,' assiduously pray to Jesus that in the day of judgment we may find mercy through thee, and receive the reward prepared by God for those who love him."* Saint John Chrysostom

My spirit rejoices in God, my Saviour

While reviewing this book in your hands, my dear reader, with one of my very dear friends, Simon, he made a captivating comment that I felt compelled not to withhold but to share with you.

Even though the word "joy" in English is amazingly simple, consisting of just three letters—J, O, and Y—it carries a profound and deep meaning. Yet, many of us struggle to truly comprehend, feel, and experience its full essence, especially when it comes to Christ Himself. Just pronouncing it brings joy to our hearts, particularly to the simple heart that does not concern itself much with life's challenges. We are too occupied and focused on the complexities of our world during our brief journey here, unlike Saint Mary, who embraced a life of simplicity and unwavering faith.

Saint Mary is regarded as the highest Saint in the Orthodox Church. She is higher than all the heavenly Saints and any man or woman saint who ever lived. She is called the Theotokos, a Greek word meaning "God-bearer," or the "Mother of God." The Coptic church focuses on the life of Saint Mary in the month of August. The fast of Saint Mary is from August 7 – August 21. The feast of the assumption of Saint Mary is August 22.

During this holy month of Kiahk in the Coptic Orthodox Church, we commemorate the events that led to the transformation of the world through the birth of our Lord Jesus Christ. We are called to be attentive and faithful during this time, for we see the Feast of the Nativity on the horizon, rapidly approaching as each day passes. It is a time for us to prepare and wait for the feast commemorating the coming of the Son of God. Saint John Chrysostom recognised the awesome significance of this feast, saying,

"A feast day is about to arrive, and it is the most holy and awesome of all feasts. It would be no mistake to call it the chief and mother of all holy days. What feast is that? It is the day of Christ's birth in the flesh."

During this month we sing many joyful hymns to glorify the immaculate birth of our Lord Jesus Christ and honour Saint Mary, the Mother of God, saying, "Rejoice O Mary, handmaiden and mother, for the angels praise Him who is on your arms."

Key lessons from Saint Mary's life

The Assumption of the Virgin Mary, the Theotokos, is a momentous occasion celebrated with reverence and joy in the hearts of believers around the church. On the 21st of the Coptic month of Touba, we commemorate the glorious Assumption of the body of our pure Lady Saint Mary the Theotokos into the heavenly realms, surrounded by the ineffable splendour of angelic hosts.

As the Synaxarium recounts, the disciples, except for Saint Thomas, who was spreading the Gospel in distant lands, gathered around the holy body of the Virgin Mary to pay their final respects and receive her divine blessings. With hearts heavy yet filled with reverence, they laid her precious form to rest in the tomb.

For three sacred days, the atmosphere surrounding her sepulchre was imbued with celestial melodies, angelic voices resounding in praise of the pure and blessed Virgin. A sweet fragrance, a tangible manifestation of her sanctity, pervaded the tomb, a testament to her exalted status in the eyes of heaven and earth.

Then, on the third day, in an event unseen by mortal eyes, the angels, in a majestic procession befitting her royal stature, bore her immaculate body to the celestial realms. There, in the presence of the Almighty, she was crowned with glory and honour. Though the disciples did not witness this heavenly ascent of their beloved Mother, their hearts were lifted up with the knowledge that she had been received into the bosom of God, where she intercedes on behalf of all humanity as the compassionate and ever-vigilant Mother of us all.

As we commemorate this sacred occasion, let us draw inspiration from the life of the Virgin Mary, whose humble obedience and unwavering faith brought forth the Saviour of the world. May her example guide us on our earthly pilgrimage, and may her intercession and prayers be a source of strength and consolation in our times of need. Amen.

Saint Mary's encounter with the Archangel Gabriel in the Annunciation holds profound lessons and joyful insights for believers. Here are three key takeaways from this passage:

1. Faith and Trust in God's Promises. Despite the seeming impossibility of the angel's message, Saint Mary responded with faith and humility, saying, "Let it be to me according to your

IN A WORLD FILLED WITH SCEPTICISM AND DISBELIEF, SAINT MARY'S FAITH TEACHES US THE IMPORTANCE OF TRUSTING GOD'S PLAN FOR OUR LIVES, EVEN WHEN IT SEEMS BEYOND OUR COMPREHENSION.

word." Her unwavering trust in God's promises, even in the face of uncertainty and doubt, serves as a powerful example for believers. Like Saint Mary, we are called to submit entirely to God's will, confident that He is faithful to fulfil His promises in His perfect timing.

2. Humility and Obedience: Saint Mary's humble acceptance of her role in God's plan exemplifies the virtues of humility and obedience. Despite her own fears and reservations, she submitted herself entirely to God's will, professing herself as the "handmaid of the Lord." Her willingness to embrace her divine calling with humility and obedience paved the way for fulfilling God's redemptive plan through the birth of our Lord Jesus Christ. Saint Mary's example challenges us to cultivate humility and obedience in our own lives, and to recognise that true greatness lies in serving God's purposes with a willing and obedient heart.

3. Rejoicing in God's Blessings: The Archangel Gabriel greeted Saint Mary with the words, "Rejoice, highly favoured one, the Lord is with you." Saint Mary's response to this divine greeting reflects her deep sense of joy and gratitude for God's blessings in her life. Despite the challenges and uncertainties she faced, Saint Mary rejoiced in the knowledge that she had found Favor with God and was

LIKE SAINT MARY, WE ARE CALLED TO CULTIVATE A SPIRIT OF JOY AND GRATITUDE, RECOGNIZING THAT EVERY GOOD GIFT COMES FROM GOD AND EMBRACING HIS BLESSINGS WITH A THANKFUL HEART.

chosen to play a signal role in His redemptive plan. Her joyful acceptance of God's will serve as a reminder to believers of the importance of rejoicing in God's blessings, even amid trials and tribulations.

In conclusion, Saint Mary's encounter with the Archangel Gabriel in the Annunciation offers us timeless lessons in faith, humility, obedience, and joy. As we reflect on her example, may we be inspired to emulate her virtues in our own lives, trusting in God's promises, humbly obeying His will, and rejoicing in His abundant blessings.

Saint Mary's profound response, "Let it be to me according to your word," epitomizes a life of submission to God's will, marked by simplicity, selflessness, and sacrificial giving. This submission brings forth true joy, contrasting with the obstacles that hinder rejoicing. Let us delve deeper into the meaning of this submission and its implications:

1. Submission Over Logic: Saint Mary's response transcends this-worldly human logic. She did not refuse the angel's extraordinary message despite its seeming impossibility but instead submitted herself entirely to God's divine plan. Similarly, in our own lives, we often face situations that defy human understanding. Rather than relying solely on our limited logic, we are called to submit to God's wisdom and trust in His unfailing guidance. Like Daniel in the lion's den, Abraham in his old age, and Moses at the Red Sea, we are challenged to relinquish our human reasoning and place our faith entirely in God's providence.

2. Identifying the obstacles to joy: Saint Mary's submission stands in stark contrast to the enemies

of rejoicing listed—logical necessity, need, anxiety, desire for success, fear, materialism, and human wisdom. These obstacles distract us from experiencing true joy by shifting our focus away from God and onto ourselves. By submitting our worries, fears, and desires to God, we can overcome these hindrances and embrace the joy that comes from trusting in His divine plan.

3. Practical Aspects of Submission: Living a life of submission involves practical steps, such as relinquishing our need for control, trusting God's provision, and abandoning pessimism and materialism. It requires us to let go of our own agendas and to embrace God's will with humility and obedience. Just as Saint Mary's submission paved the way, from the human side, for the moment of the Incarnation, so also our own submission opens the door to God's transformative work in our lives.

Saint Mary's response exemplifies the beauty and power of submission to God's will. Through this submission that we find true joy, unencumbered by the obstacles and distractions of this world. As we follow Saint Mary's example, may we, too, say, "Let it be to me according to your word," and experience the abundant joy that comes from living in alignment with God's divine plan.

Do not worry about the future

Remember, if we walk with our Lord, we will lack nothing. Keep in mind Psalm 23, "The Lord is my shepherd, I shall not want, even though I walk through the valley of the shadow of death, I will fear no evil, for You are with me" (Psalm

23:4). Remember and believe that He will be with us, the one who started the journey with us cannot leave us.

We must submit ourselves entirely to God. Look how much God loved Saint Paul. Yet He did say of him, "I will show him how many things he must suffer for My name's sake" (Acts 9:16). This does not mean that if we experience pain and tribulation in our life, God does not love us. On the contrary, He loves us very much and specifically allows us the pain. Did not our Lord love Saint Mary? Yet it was said to her, "A sword will pierce through your own soul" (Luke 2:35). Did not the Lord love Saint George, yet He allowed him to suffer for seven years and be tortured? With the pain, there is a gift; this is true.

The future of my life, my family, my children is to be trusted to God and be genuinely believed in. He said to Joshua, "As I was with Moses, so I will be with you. I will not leave you nor forsake you" (Joshua 1:5). In the Gospel of Saint Matthew, our Lord promised us a true and faithful promise, "I am with you always, even to the end of the age" (Chapter 28:20).

Do not worry, therefore, about the future. You cannot change a single strand of hair from your head, so please do not be anxious. Do not try to secure the future by yourself. We are extremely limited; therefore, we should leave it to the unlimited. If we try to secure money, money will not be able to secure health; if we secure health, we will not be able to secure favourable circumstances; if we secure favourable circumstances, we will not be able to secure nature; if we secure nature, we will not be able to secure governments that are floundering in this world; if we secure governments, we will not be able to secure the global economy; and if we secure the global economy, we will not be able to prevent wars in the world. There are so many variables in our lives beyond our imagination that we cannot change.

Remember that our best support and protection is in our Lord Jesus. He said, "Come to me, all you who are weary and are heavily burdened, and I will give you rest" (Matthew 11:28); "He who dwells in the secret place of the Most High, shall abide under the shadow of the Almighty. I will say of the Lord, "He is my refuge and my fortress; My God, in Him I will trust" (Psalm 91:1-2). Everything in God's hands is secured thereby.

Be optimistic in Christ, "My Father has been working until now, and I have been working" (Luke 5:17). You will never wake up in the morning and not see the rising sun, you will never find a bird without food to eat or that has died from hunger, you will never wake up one day and discover that there is no more food in the world... therefore, always remain positive and look to God, who secures everything in our life... is what is meant by, "Let it be according to Your word," this is submission, with practical steps to understand.

Another key to joyful life: Saint Mary's life of simplicity,

Another key to joy is the simplicity of life that Saint Mary lived. Nowadays, we live in an overly complex and sophisticated society. Simplicity means not comparing yourself with others, not comparing your children or grandchildren with others, and not comparing your circumstances with others. Avoid looking around you and over your shoulder at others too much. Be happy, satisfied and content with what you have and with what God has provided you with. Always thank your Lord, on every occasion, in every condition and for all things, and just remember that we do not deserve anything at all. Try to be joyful and grateful, enjoying everything from the hand of God.

Enjoy the talents that God has given you. Saint Mary, the simple Virgin, went and served and invested her talents. Rejoice in nature and in the creation around you. Enjoy the day, enjoy even a simple cup of tea and the food we eat. It is a blessing from God. Thank God for your health even if you have an illness, stay simple in your calculations and your ambitions, simple in the analysis of things, straightforward in your words, and do not be too sensitive when receiving sharp words from another person. Do not dwell too much on these words.

Turn your life around instead, be simple, and stay away from complexity. You will then begin to know joy, and There was something beautiful and powerful in Saint Mary. Although she was simple and submitted her life and said, "Let it be according to Your word Lord," she did not hold on to anything in this world, not even her only Son when he mounted the Cross and gave His life for the entire world. It is entirely fitting, therefore, that we should say to her, "Rejoice, O Mary, Mother and Virgin." She has an immensely powerful joy that anyone who seeks her prayers will rejoice.

> WHEN YOU PUT EVERYTHING IN GOD'S HANDS, YOU WILL REJOICE EVEN MORE.

Final words

Chapter 11 probed into the profound significance of submission and simplicity, drawing inspiration from the life of Saint Mary, the Mother of God. Through reflections on her obedience, trust, and joyful submission to God's will, readers are invited to embrace a life marked by submission to divine providence and the beauty of simplicity. As we contemplate Saint Mary's example, may her virtues inspire us to cultivate a spirit of humility, trust, and joy in our own lives, finding solace and strength in submitting to God's perfect plan.

Questions for Self-reflection:

1. How does Saint Mary's response to the angel Gabriel challenge your understanding of submission and obedience to God's will?

2. Reflect on a time when you struggled to submit to God's plan for your life. What barriers or obstacles prevented you from fully submitting to His will?

3. Consider the role of simplicity in your life. In what areas do you find it challenging to maintain a simple and contented outlook?

4. Saint Mary's life exemplifies joyful submission to God's will, even in the face of uncertainty and sacrifice. How can you cultivate a similar spirit of joy and trust in your own journey of faith?

5. Reflect on the obstacles to joy listed in the chapter—logic, need, anxiety, desire for success, fear, materialism, and human wisdom. Which of these and similar obstacles do you struggle with the most, and how can you overcome them?

6. Consider the practical aspects of submission discussed in the chapter. What steps can you take to relinquish control and trust more fully in God's providence in your daily life?

7. Saint Mary's simplicity and selflessness serve as powerful examples for believers. How can you emulate her virtues in your relationships, your attitudes toward possessions, and your daily interactions with others?

May we all be joyful and may joy prevail in our lives and may we overcome the complexities and problems in our lives. If something depletes us in our life, seek the Virgin Saint Mary, and she will support us.

Chapter 12

Savouring Joy in Suffering: Insights from Psalm 34

"Keep the psalms in your heart, and they will keep you."
Pope Shenouda III

The mighty weapon of praying the Psalms

The message of this simple yet profound saying of the timeless Pope Shenouda III, our inspiring and encouraging companion during the journey of our book, is that praying the Psalms offers us a unique and fervent joy, a comfort that resonates deeply within our hearts. These ancient holy songs of prayer and praise, of repentance and supplication, embrace the full spectrum of human emotions, from despair to elation, from total need to jubilation. As we recite these sacred verses, we tap a wellspring of divine wisdom and solace; we are educated in a profound connection with God.

> THEY ACT UPON US TO BRING A RICHNESS OF HEALING AND OF PEACE TO OUR SPIRITUAL LIVES.

King David, the revered author of many Psalms, wrote and sang these hymns from the depths of his own wealth and rich experiences. His life was marked by extraordinary triumphs and devastating lows, and through it all, he turned to God in prayer and song. The Psalms reflect his heartfelt cries, his jubilant praises, and his unwavering faith. By praying the Psalms, we join David in his spiritual journey, finding comfort in his words and drawing strength from his example. These sacred texts not only articulate our deepest longings and fears but also provide a pathway to experience the overwhelming joy of God's presence, guiding us toward a life filled with spiritual abundance and tranquillity.

In this chapter, let us pause with Psalm 34 for a while, to learn what we may as we continue our journey seeking the keys of inner joy.

"I will bless the Lord at all times; His praise shall continually be in my mouth. My soul shall make its boast in the Lord; the humble shall hear of it and be glad. Oh, magnify the Lord with me, and let us exalt His name together. I sought the Lord, and He heard me, and delivered me from all my fears. They looked to Him and were radiant, and their faces were not ashamed.

Savouring Joy in Suffering: Insights from Psalm 34

This poor man cried out, and the Lord heard him, and saved him out of all his troubles. The angel of the Lord encamps all around those who fear Him, And delivers them. Oh, taste and see that the Lord is good; Blessed is the man who trusts in Him! Oh, fear the Lord, you His saints! There is no want to those who fear Him. The young lions lack and suffer hunger; But those who seek the Lord shall not lack any good thing. Come, you children, listen to me; I will teach you the fear of the Lord.

Who is the man who desires life, and loves many days, that he may see good? Keep your tongue from evil, and your lips from speaking deceit. Depart from evil and do good; Seek peace and pursue it.

The eyes of the Lord are on the righteous, and His ears are open to their cry. The face of the Lord is against those who do evil, to cut off the remembrance of them from the earth. The righteous cry out, and the Lord hears, and delivers them out of all their troubles. The Lord is near to those who have a broken heart, and saves such as have a contrite spirit. Many are the afflictions of the righteous; But the Lord delivers him out of them all.

He guards all his bones; not one of them is broken. Evil shall slay the wicked, And those who hate the righteous shall be condemned. The Lord redeems the soul of His servants, And none of those who trust in Him shall be condemned. Alleluia" (Psalm 34).

An invitation: taste the beauty of the Lord!

The beauty of this Psalm lies in its deep connection to King David's heartfelt personal experience. "Oh, taste and see that the Lord is good. Blessed is the man who trusts in Him" (Psalm 34:8). David penned this Psalm after escaping from Ahimelech and fleeing to Achish, the King of Gath. To avoid danger, he altered his behaviour and feigned madness before the king, leading to his expulsion.

King David went to the Philistines twice. The first time, he was accompanied by several of his men (1 Samuel 21). He was petrified when he returned to Gath, the city where he had killed Goliath, carrying Goliath's sword with him. The Philistines were eager to find David and kill him, as many widows and orphans had been affected at that time because he had killed many of the Philistines with the sword of Goliath. They suspected him of being a spy, coming from Saul. So, David pretended to be a madman before the King, and scratched at the doors of the gate and let saliva run down his beard. Achish then said to his servants, "Look, you see the man is insane. Why have you brought him to me?" (1 Samuel 21:14). The second time, David went to Gath with 600 soldiers, men who were persecuted, and found a way to help them. The king welcomed him and gave him a city, Ziklag, to live in.

The purpose of sharing this story with you, dear

WHEN ONE LOSES EVERYTHING, OR IS IN GREAT NEED, OR IN SEVERE PAIN, THEY CAN TRULY EXPERIENCE THE SWEETNESS AND GOODNESS OF OUR LORD'S WORK IN THEIR LIFE.

reader, is to underscore that when King David wrote the words, "Oh, taste and see that the Lord is good" (Psalm 34:8), he was at a very weak and vulnerable point in his life. He was extremely distressed, having been expelled and experienced failure. He did not enjoy any pleasures, nor did he live in a palace. Instead, he was a fugitive, on the run, anxious, in pain, having lost everything. Yet, despite all this, David still wrote these words.

Key themes and lessons from the Psalmist

Psalm 34 offers profound insights into the nature of inner joy, particularly amid adversity and trials. Let us explore some key themes and reflections inspired by this Psalm:

1. Continuous Praise and Trust: The Psalm begins with a declaration of perpetual praise and trust in the Lord, regardless of circumstances. King David resolves to always bless the Lord and he praises Him continually. This attitude of unwavering trust and praise reflects a deep-seated confidence in God's goodness and faithfulness.

2. Divine Deliverance: king David testifies to the Lord's faithfulness in delivering him from all his fears and troubles. He recounts his firsthand experiences of seeking the Lord and finding refuge in Him. This narrative of divine deliverance serves as a source of encouragement and hope for believers facing their own trials and challenges.

3. *Taste and See*: The Psalm invites readers *to taste and see the goodness of the Lord*, emphasising the

experiential aspect of faith. King David's exhortation to taste and see that the Lord is good implies a personal encounter with God's goodness and a transformative experience of His presence.

4. The Fear of the Lord: Again, King David instructs his listeners in the fear of the Lord, acknowledging the blessings and protection that come to those who honour and revere God. This fear of the Lord is not rooted in dread or terror but in reverence and awe, leading to a life of willing obedience, loyalty and righteousness.

5. The Promise of Deliverance: The Psalm reassures believers of God's nearness to the broken hearted and His commitment to deliverance. King David acknowledges the reality of afflictions the righteous face but affirms God's faithfulness in delivering them from all their troubles.

6. Personal Testimony: Finally, Psalm 34 concludes with a personal testimony of redemption and salvation. King David proclaims the Lord's faithfulness in redeeming the souls of His servants and assures that none who trust in Him will be condemned.

In sum, Psalm 34 serves as a powerful testament to the transformative power of faith and trust in God's goodness, even amid adversity. King David's individual experiences of divine deliverance and redemption offer encouragement and hope to believers, inspiring them to praise God continually and trust in His unfailing love and protection.

Savouring Joy in Suffering: Insights from Psalm 34

The intertwining of pain and joy

The intertwining of pain and joy in human experience is a profound mystery. Both pain and joy are cantered in the soul, resonating within us in diverse ways, reflecting the multi-layered depths of our soul's journey.

In moments of pain, we often find ourselves bowed down, humbled by the weight of our struggles and uncertainties. The psalmist's lament, "Why are you cast down, O my soul?" (Ps 42:11) expresses our own inner turmoil, urging us to confront our own vulnerabilities and weaknesses. This bowing down brings us close to the earth. Where then, does joy in the midst of pain come from?

In this humbling process, in this experience of the rawness of human suffering, we are drawn closer to the compassionate heart of our Lord Jesus Christ. In this closeness to our Lord Jesus Christ, we discover the source of true joy amidst our pain. By fixing our gaze upon Jesus, the author and finisher of our faith, we learn to navigate the valleys of suffering with hope and resilience, "Looking unto Jesus, the author and finisher of our faith, who for the joy that was set before Him endured the cross, despising the shame" (Hebrews 12:2). Just as Mary the sister of Martha sat at His feet and drew closer to Him, absorbing His teachings and presence, we too can draw near to Him in our moments of trial. The closer we get to the earth, the nearer we come to those suffering, and the closer we will be to Jesus Christ, who said, "Blessed are those who mourn for they will rejoice" (Matthew 5:4).

When we are close to Christ, we meditate on Him and learn from Him, "Looking unto Jesus, the author and finisher of our faith, who for the joy that was set before Him endured the cross, despising the shame" (Hebrews 12:2. Mary the sister of Martha sat at His feet gathering up his words and drawing closer to Him. Many sold all they had and lived a simple, poor life in the wilderness, like Saint Anthony, just to be with Him. Multitudes went after Jesus to hear Him, and they drew closer to Him; they received joy by being close to Christ. Christ brings a beautiful taste, comfort, warmth, joy, and pleasure to the soul. The closer we are to Christ, the more we find fulfilment and joy. It is hard to explain; one must live it and experience it for oneself. In pain we come to taste Christ more and to rejoice in Him more. We feel more deeply every word in the liturgy and in Scripture.

The Lord is very close to us in suffering

This explains that often there are no words to console those who are suffering, to make them happy, because they are with Christ, in His embrace, in His tenderness and in His love. You want to give advice when a person is in pain or sick or experiencing tribulation, but often it is better not to speak or give suggestions or to say this problem is simple and will go

IN SUFFERING, THE LORD IS BOTH EXTREMELY NEAR AND MORE COMPASSIONATE. HE FEELS OUR PAINS AND TAKES US INTO HIS EMBRACE, AND IT IS THEN THAT WE FEEL THE INNER JOY.

away, or it will be better tomorrow. Do not send links to sermons because the person at present is broken from inside. Such attempts may be sincere and genuine, but sometimes silence is better, and then the suffering person will acknowledge your feelings and your presence beside them and that you are nearby to help them at any time.

The suffering soul is ascetic. It has no pleasures in life and does not desire to eat, buy, listen, or see. Take this as a rule: the more this world decreases, the more the soul becomes ascetic, and the Lord is magnified within us. The more we leave this world, the more we take the hand of our Lord and, the more we shall come to feel Him, and the more we shall rejoice, because all joy is centred in our Lord; its gift and its source is from him.

Do not expect to find true inner joy in the world. You will not find it, and you will be disappointed. The suffering person is lost in an ocean of pain, has lost their direction, their orientation, their logic, their balance. They have lost many things and are trying to grasp at little straws to cling to Christ and abide in Him. Seek to attend liturgies and give yourself to prayer, for indeed, our Lord is our refuge and our protector. So then, let us do as David said, "I have set the Lord always before me" (Psalm 16:8).

When we put all our hope in Christ, we become like incense in the censer, which is kindled by fire and gives off a beautiful aroma. So, Suffering and pain always generate true inner joy. We discover a profound

WE ARE DRAWN TO COME CLOSE TO A SICK AND SUFFERING PERSON BECAUSE THEY HAVE THE SCENT OF CHRIST.

truth: that in the crucible of pain, our souls are made receptive to the beauty and richness of Christ's love. Every word of Scripture, every note of the Liturgy, becomes imbued with new meaning and significance for us, resonating deeply within our hearts.

The joy discovered in the midst of pain does not come from fleeting pleasures or momentary happiness but from the enduring grace of Christ's presence. It is a joy that sustains us through the darkest of nights and lifts us to new heights of spiritual understanding. As we immerse ourselves in His love, we find that even amidst the trials of life, our souls are filled with an abiding sense of peace and contentment.

My beloved sufferer who walks in life carrying your cross, trust that your pain will turn into inner joy with the Lord Jesus Christ if you are not seeking it from the world.

Final words

In Chapter 12, we delved into the profound insights of Psalm 34, exploring the theme of finding joy in the midst of suffering. Through the lens of King David's firsthand experiences, we uncovered the transformative power of trust, praise, and intimacy with God, even amidst the most severe and challenging circumstances. This chapter illuminated the paradoxical mingling of joy and suffering, revealing how pain can serve as a gateway to deeper spiritual communion and inner joy in the presence of the Lord.

Questions for self-reflection:

1. How does the testimony of King David in Psalm 34 challenge your perspective on suffering and joy?

2. Reflect on a time of personal hardship or adversity. In what ways did you experience the presence and goodness of God amid your suffering?

3. Consider your response to suffering. Do you find yourself seeking comfort primarily from worldly sources, or do you turn to God for solace and strength?

4. King David found solace and redemption in his moments of weakness and vulnerability. How can you cultivate a deeper sense of trust and intimacy with God during times of suffering?

5. Reflect on the concept of joy rooted in Christ's presence rather than in worldly pleasures. How can you shift your focus from temporary happiness to enduring joy found in communion with God?

Chapter 13

Embracing Joy in the midst of tribulations

> "He who endures distress, will be granted joys; and he who bears with unpleasant things, will not be deprived of the pleasant." St. Nilus of Sinai

Misunderstanding God's purpose of suffering

The teachings of our Lord Jesus Christ in the Sermon on the Mount hold immense importance and possess a captivating power of transformation for any human being who earnestly seeks to live by them. They contain the deepest and most valuable principles that Christians should constantly reflect upon, revisit, and embody in this world. Each of these teachings is like a precious jewel, and when combined, they form the very foundation of Christianity.

Allow me to share an inspiring story about a university professor who, despite not overtly discussing or preaching about Christianity or giving sermons or talks, nevertheless exemplified its essence through living his life as a true salt of the earth and light to the world.

When once questioned by his students in the university auditorium about his faith, he humbly revealed that he may not be an avid reader of the Bible or someone who prays a lot. Still, every morning before leaving his house, he would read three chapters from the Gospel of Saint Matthew, specifically chapters 5, 6, and 7 - the Sermon on the Mount. This simple practice became his secret recipe for cultivating a strong Christian life that radiated God's love. He truly embodied being the salt of the earth and the light of the world. Upon hearing this story many years ago, my appreciation for the Sermon on the Mount grew immensely. I began to read and revisit its teachings regularly, finding solace, inspiration, and guidance within its words.

Recently, while I was absorbed in authoring this book about joy, a profound realisation struck me. The only instance the word "joy" appears in the Sermon on the Mount is when our Lord Jesus teaches, "Blessed are you when they persecute you... rejoice!" The Sermon on the Mount encompasses the highest level of teaching from our Lord Jesus Christ. Its

IT IS AS IF GOD HIMSELF IS REVEALING THAT TRUE JOY IS BESTOWED UPON US WHEN WE WHOLEHEARTEDLY ACCEPT AND PERSEVERE THROUGH TRIBULATIONS.

teachings, like rare and precious gems, hold the power to transform our lives and shape our understanding of true joy. May we continually embrace and live out these teachings, becoming beacons of light and agents of love in this world.

In his epistle, Saint James the Apostle makes an unusual statement, "My brethren, count it all joy when you fall into various trials" (James 1:2). Many years ago, I would read this verse and hear sermons on it, but I would never feel its impact or understand it or interact with it. Trials? What does that mean? Sickness, death, material losses, failure, persecution? Count them all joy? Maximum joy? How?

We have readily believed that happiness stems from a beautiful and peaceful world, where everything remains calm and undisturbed. We find joy when there is no turmoil, no waves crashing against our boat, and everything is proceeding smoothly. However, our church teaches us a profoundly different truth. The Scriptures reveal a counterpoint on true joy. Our Church rites instruct us to pray in a joyful tune during the month of Tout, which marks the beginning of the Coptic New Year of Martyrs, continuing until the Feast of the Cross on the 19th of Tout. This practice teaches us that the time of the martyrs and the time of the Cross is a time of joy.

In the month of Tout, we are reminded that joy is not merely the absence of difficulty but the coming of God's grace and strength amid trials. The martyrs' unwavering faith and the victory of the Cross exemplify a joy that transcends earthly circumstances. This sacred period invites us to embrace a deeper, more resilient joy that flourishes even in the face of adversity. Through our Church's teachings, we learn that true joy is found in our steadfast faith and the transformative power of God's love, even when the seas of life are turbulent.

Why, then do we rejoice in trials? It is essential to recognise that Satan, the father of lies, plants the deceitful notion in our minds that the God we follow is cruel. This often leads us to question, "How can a loving God allow us to suffer pain?" Such thoughts can easily take root, causing us to lose sight of the blessings, joy, and comfort that can come from suffering. Instead, we become self-centred; we think that we are victims, asking, "Why has God chosen me to experience this pain? Why not others who seem to have it easier, with their families and good health?"

Such a mindset weakens our perception of the Holy Spirit's work within us and allows Satan to build a wall between us and God. When we dwell on these thoughts, we miss the divine purpose and growth that can come from our trials. Rejoicing in trials does not mean we ignore our pain; rather, it means we trust that God is at work in our suffering, refining our faith and drawing us closer to Him.

Our trials are opportunities for spiritual growth and a deeper reliance on God. They teach us to look beyond our immediate circumstances and find strength in His presence. By shifting our focus from "Why me?" to "What is God teaching me through this?" we begin to see our trials as a path to greater faith and joy. We remember that God's love and sovereignty are steadfast, even amid our struggles.

Pain is not God's anger towards us. God was not angry with Christ when He suffered on the Cross, or with Saint Paul, or Saint Mary, or Saint George, or all the beautiful believers who have suffered.

Yet pain helps save and regenerate us. Contemplate the potter who presses hard on the clay between his fingers while it is on the turntable to shape it. The clay is then placed in the oven at extremely high temperatures for it to dry and become a beautiful vase or other precious item, and then it is sold at an exceedingly high price. Pain is exactly like this; it is not for our hurt. Christ came to suffer with me and to share in my suffering and this is a sign of his love. In the Liturgy of St. Gregory, we pray, "You have turned for me the punishment into salvation." Hence, pain becomes a path to perfection, even as happened with Job.

Pain is like the scalpel a surgeon uses to remove a bad lesion from a patient so that he becomes good as new. The presence of pain allows us to grow spiritually, to share with Him, "That I may know Him and the fellowship of His sufferings" (Philippians 3:10). The path of pain is the path all the Saints who have loved the Lord and taken the royal road of his Cross. One of these Saints has said that three things take us on the path to our Lord: sickness, death, and voluntary poverty. Which John Piper sums up beautifully as: "This is God's universal purpose for all Christian suffering: more contentment in God and less satisfaction in the world."

Why does God allow us to suffer?

To reject the love of the world and hate the sin that caused the pain, let us fall into the arms of Christ, who can purify and cleanse us from every sin by His Blood. Trials wean the person from loving the world, like a mother putting myrrh on her baby's finger to deter the baby from putting its finger in its mouth. However, the strange and beautiful thing is that, amid all the trials, God gives comfort, patience, and endurance, "His left hand is under my head, and his right hand embraces me" (Song of Songs 2:6).

Saint Paul teaches us, "For as the sufferings of Christ abound in us, so our consolation also abounds through Christ" (2 Corinthians 1:5). A fellowship takes place between us and Christ, a fellowship of suffering and of consolation, a feeling of closeness to Christ where we will find comfort and inner joy. At times, we will feel weak, but most of the time, we will have fellowship with Him and remain strong and confident.

> WHEN A PERSON REJOICES AMID TRIALS, IT IS A SIGN OF LOVE, A SIGN OF PURIFICATION FROM OUR LORD, AND A SHARE OF SUFFERING FOR THE ETERNAL GLORY THAT WILL BE INHERITED AND AMPLIFIES OUR COMFORT.

We are not speaking of the joy found in the world or of laughter. No, we are speaking here of the inner joy of our souls, the joy that comes from "The peace of God, which surpasses all understanding" (Philippians 4:7), the joy of all contentment, submission, gratitude, and thanksgiving, that flows from God in a way that cannot be described.

King David said in his Psalm, "Oh taste and see that the Lord is good, blessed is the man who trusts in Him" (Psalm 34:8). Blessed is the person who trusts God and casts their burden upon our Lord. Blessed is the person who thanks God amid trials and in pain. How great it is to thank God, preaching and glorifying Him. At times, we do not thank God with our lips, but with our eyes and an accepting face, convinced,

"The Lord is my portion" (Lamentations 3:24). Yes, there is still pain and suffering for the human soul, but there is also fellowship with Christ. Joy in suffering is a great theme we have not completely covered yet. We will continue this topic in the coming chapter.

Final words

Chapter 13 explored the concept of embracing joy amidst tribulations, drawing insights from biblical passages and the teachings of the Church Fathers. It challenged the conventional understanding of joy, emphasising that true inner joy can be found even amid trials and suffering. By shifting our perspective to see pain as a path to purification and spiritual growth, we can experience a profound sense of fellowship with Christ and find comfort in His presence. The chapter underscored the transformative power of joy rooted in trust and gratitude, highlighting the paradoxical nature of finding joy amidst adversity.

Questions for self-reflection:

1. How does your understanding of joy align with the teachings of Scripture and the Church regarding suffering and trials?

2. Reflect on a time when you experienced joy amid tribulations. What lessons did you learn about God's presence and faithfulness during that season?

3. Consider your response to pain and suffering. Do you view them as opportunities for spiritual growth and fellowship with Christ, or do you struggle to find joy amidst adversity?

4. Think about the role of gratitude in cultivating inner joy. How can you cultivate a spirit of thankfulness, even amid challenging circumstances?

5. Reflect on the thought of fellowship with Christ in suffering. How can you deepen your relationship with Him during times of trials, drawing strength and comfort from His presence?

Chapter 14

The Paradox of Joy amid Suffering

> *"In the beginning there is struggle and a lot of work for those who come near to God. But after that there is indescribable joy. It is just like building a fire: at first it is smoky and your eyes water, but later you get the desired result. Thus, we ought to light the divine fire in ourselves with tears and effort."* Amma Syncletica of Alexandria

Honouring Peter: A true Story of Resilience and the Power of the Human Spirit

I fell in love with the above saying of the renowned Desert Mother Amma Syncletica of Alexandria which likens the journey to God to the labour necessary for starting a fire: initially, there is much toil and effort, but eventually, there's indescribable joy. He illustrates that just as a fire begins with being smoky and we teary-eyed, the eventual result is worth the initial discomfort. Similarly, our journey to God may start with tears and toilsome effort, but it leads to profound joy.

In a hospital ward at Sydney Prince of Wales hospital at Randwick, I witnessed a remarkable and heartwarming encounter between our much loved late son-in-law Mark, and Peter, who was a highly intellectual pharmacist who served his local pharmacy's community in utmost love and dedication. Peter's thirst for knowledge and love for reading made him a rare gem in life. Despite being paralysed and confined to a bed after a truly horrific car accident driving back home after a busy day at his pharmacy, Peter's spirit remained unbroken.

One day, at Mark's request, I accompanied him on a visit to Peter. Mark eagerly yearned to serve the Lord during the final year of his short and cherished life. As soon as they began talking together, their laughter filled the whole ward, spreading joy to everyone around them, both patients and even the nurses. It was incredible to see how they discovered humour in the circumstances. It generated an uplifting atmosphere in the hospital. I sat nearby, observing their infectious laughter and I could not restrain the big radiant smile on my face as I listened to Peter giving invaluable life lessons to Mark with incredible humour.

I wondered what was the magic of their connection.

Mark, who was always eager to help others, to serve them without a second thought, found himself being served by Peter, the paraplegic. It was a beautiful display of kindness and selflessness. The time passed, and I reluctantly reminded Mark of our other commitments, not knowing that it would be the last time we saw Peter alive.

The memory of that laughter-filled encounter in the hospital remains etched in my heart. It served as a reminder of the power of human connection and the strength of the human spirit in the face of adversity. Despite his physical limitations, Peter shared a bond with Mark that transcended his challenging, bedbound circumstances.

Though Peter departed to heaven only a few days after this grace-filled encounter, his legacy lives on. The brief but profound interaction between Mark and Peter taught us the importance of finding joy amid hardship and of extending kindness to others. As we navigate the grief of losing Mark, we hold onto the memory of that special encounter, cherishing the lessons learned and the laughter shared.

In the end, the story is a testament to the resilience of the human spirit and the power of laughter to brighten even the darkest moments. May the memory of Mark and Peter laughing together at their last meeting comfort and inspire us to embrace life's joys and to forge meaningful connections with others.

The paradox of suffering and joy mingled together

In his Second Epistle to the Corinthians, Saint Paul says, "But we have this treasure in earthen vessels, that the excellence of the power may be of God and not of us. We are hard-pressed on every side, yet not crushed; we are perplexed, but not in despair; persecuted, but not forsaken; struck down, but not destroyed— always carrying about in the body the dying of the Lord Jesus, that the life of Jesus also may be manifested in our body.

For our light affliction, which is but for a moment, is working for us a far more exceeding and eternal weight of glory, while we do not look at the things which are seen, but at the things which are not seen. For the things which are seen are temporary, but the things which are not seen are eternal" (2 Corinthians 4:7-18).

THEREFORE WE DO NOT LOSE HEART. EVEN THOUGH OUR OUTWARD MAN IS PERISHING, YET THE INWARD MAN IS BEING RENEWED DAY BY DAY.

In his Second Epistle to the Corinthians, Saint Paul articulates the paradoxical mingling of suffering and joy. He speaks of being hard-pressed, perplexed, persecuted, and struck down, yet not crushed, despairing, forsaken, or destroyed. Yet, despite the trials, there is an underlying sense of victory and resilience, attributing this endurance to the life of Jesus manifested within. He emphasizes that while outwardly we may face affliction, inwardly, we are renewed day by day, focusing on the eternal rather than the temporal.

Here, Saint Paul directs our attention to death, "So then death is working in us, but life in you" (2 Corinthians 4:12). A mother who is in labour bears the pain so she can give birth to her child. Childbirth is so difficult because the mother is attached to her child, with the picture of her newborn baby and her dreams in front of her, granting her joy from within. She knows the things which are not seen, the baby, and though experiencing pain, she underestimates everything that is coming: the sleepless nights, the breastfeeding, neglecting herself and her health, not pursuing her own dreams or convenience. Instead, everything is centred on this child. She puts all her efforts into this service. This child will grow and perhaps will not appreciate her, yet for now, she concentrates on the things which are not seen, and amid her pains, she is fully content and happy, glad to sacrifice herself that a new life may brought into the light, whole and entire.

Saint Paul's words echo the experience of childbirth, where the pain is endured for the joy of a new life. Similarly, he rejoices in his sufferings, understanding that they contribute to the growth and transformation of others. He finds joy amid pain, recognising the redemptive purpose behind his trials.

It is a joy born amid pain, akin to a candle burning bright despite its gradual diminishment. In embracing suffering, we embrace the opportunity to partake in Christ's redemptive work and share in His glory.

This is the pain that yields joy. While imprisoned, Saint Paul said, "I rejoice in my pain." This joy is born amid pain, which is exactly like a mother's labour pains, brings inner joy, gratitude, peace, comfort, contentment,

THIS PARADOXICAL JOY STEMS FROM SHARING IN OUR LORD CHRIST'S SUFFERINGS, A PARTICIPATION THAT BRINGS ABOUT A PROFOUND SENSE OF FULFILMENT AND CONTENTMENT.

and safety. Truly, there is death in the body. Still, there is birth, death but life, pain but reborn joy, and someone dissolves or burns like the candle that burns but brings light, the light of Jesus.

This is the highest and most inspirational level of joy because we share the sufferings of Christ and complete Christ's afflictions for the sake of His glory. Blessed is the person who lives in these circumstances. The most challenging part here is ensuring we do not focus too much on ourselves. Be sure that Christ hears, observes, and sees, and He says to us, "I know your works, your labour, your patience, and long sufferings." (Revelation 2:2)

Focussing on self, an obstacle and a battle

The challenge lies in not becoming consumed by self-focus but rather in maintaining faith and endurance. Our Lord and Saviour Jesus Christ sees our labour, patience, and long-suffering, promising to be with us through every trial. As we navigate the paradox of suffering and joy, may we find comfort in knowing that our trials serve a higher purpose and lead to a deeper union with Christ.

Though the path may be marked by blood, tears, and pain, it leads to an inheritance of unimaginable splendour. Every trial endured on

THE GLORY AND THE JOY THAT AWAITS THOSE WHO ENDURE SUFFERING FOR THEIR FAITH IS BEYOND COMPARE.

earth will pale in comparison to the eternal joy that awaits. Those who suffer for Christ can look forward to an eternity free from tears and pain, where their scarred Savior will be their everlasting delight.

Enduring suffering with joy, as the saints of old did, sets a powerful example for others. Your steadfast faith and commitment to the gospel will be admired, and God will be glorified as He sanctifies and strengthens your faith through the refining fires of affliction.

Final words

In this chapter, we explored the paradoxical nature of joy amidst suffering, drawing inspiration from the teachings of Amma Syncletica and Saint Paul the Apostle. Amma Syncletica beautifully likened the journey to God to starting a fire, where initial struggle and effort give way to indescribable joy. Saint Paul, in his letters to the Corinthians and Colossians, echoed this sentiment, emphasising the transformative power of suffering and the profound joy found in sharing in Christ's afflictions.

Despite facing constant trials and tribulations, Saint Paul remained steadfast in his faith, finding joy amid pain and recognising the redemptive purpose behind his sufferings. He understood that just as a mother endures the pangs of childbirth for the joy of new life, so too does our suffering lead to spiritual growth and transformation.

This paradoxical joy, born amid pain, is a testimony to our participation in Christ's redemptive work and His glory. It is a reminder that while there may be death in the body, there is also rebirth and new life. As we navigate life's challenges, may we remain focused on Christ, knowing He sees and acknowledges our efforts. Our trials serve a higher purpose, leading us to a deeper union with Him and bringing about everlasting joy.

Questions for Self-reflection:

1. Have you experienced moments of joy amidst suffering in your own life? If so, what lessons did you learn from those experiences?

2. How does Amma Syncletica analogy of starting a fire and Saint Paul's teachings on suffering resonate with your understanding of spirituality?

3. In what ways can you shift your perspective during times of difficulty to focus more on the eternal rather than the temporary?

4. What steps can you take to cultivate a deeper sense of joy and resilience in the face of adversity, drawing inspiration from the examples of Saint Paul and other spiritual leaders?

5. How can you ensure that your focus remains on Christ rather than becoming consumed by self-focus during challenging times?

Chapter 15

Braving the Obstacles to Christian Joy

> This rejoicing is not separable from grief, for indeed it is deeply connected with grief. The one who grieves for his own wrongdoing and confesses it is joyful. Alternatively, it is possible to grieve for one's own sins but to rejoice in Christ.... On this account he says, "Rejoice in the Lord." For this is nothing if you have received a life worthy of rejoicing.... He is right to repeat himself. For since the events are naturally grievous, it is through the repetition that he shows that one should rejoice in all cases. Saint John Chrysostom

Questions to be answered

What are the impediments that hinder the experience of joy in our lives?

In life, I believe that to address any obstacle effectively, one must dig deep into the roots of the problem to reach a precise and accurate diagnosis. The greatest obstacle to living a joyful life lies within our own selves, in our profound negligence and ignorance of the fact that true joy exists with God. By failing to recognise this divine source of joy, we often seek fulfilment in temporary and superficial pleasures that leave us feeling empty and dissatisfied.

Let me remind you, my dear reader: Only when we acknowledge and embrace this truth can we overcome the world's superficial distractions and experience the fullness of joy that God offers us. Through spiritual growth, obedience, worship, and gratitude, we can cultivate this joy and allow it to permeate every aspect of our lives, transforming our hearts and minds.

> TRUE JOY IS NOT MERELY A PASSING EMOTION OR A FLEETING STATE OF HAPPINESS; IT IS A PROFOUND, ENDURING SENSE OF CONTENTMENT AND PEACE THAT COMES FROM A DEEP, INTIMATE RELATIONSHIP WITH OUR CREATOR.

I recently had the privilege of being invited to a retreat for young Christian families, a group of beautiful families in the preliminary stages of their lives. With adorable kids in tow, these families were working tirelessly to strike a balance between their Christian beliefs and values and the challenges of a competitive world that is pushing against their direction.

As the sole speaker at the conference, I had the opportunity to delve into the topic of joy. In my first session, I posed a thought-provoking question to the group: "How would you define joy? Tell me about your experiences of joy in your lives." The room buzzed with anticipation as everyone shared their thoughts, hoping to uncover the essence of joy. However, as the discussion went on, it became apparent that many felt a void when it came to understanding joy. One courageous soul finally admitted, "We do not know joy. We have not experienced it, and we honestly do not know what you are talking about."

At that moment, I realised the magnitude of the task before us as servants of the Lord. It saddened me to think that Christians, who should be beacons of joy, often struggle to find it in their own lives. Yet, this realization also kindled in me a deep sense of responsibility. It became clear that it was our duty to help people discover the joy that exists should they choose to seek God and embrace it.

This retreat was a profound reminder of the weight on our shoulders as servants of the Lord. It has reinforced the importance for me of spreading the message of joy, of guiding others towards the path where they can truly experience the abundant joy that God offers. Together, let us embark on this journey, sharing the joy waiting to be discovered by all who seek it.

Here then, are further questions to be addressed: how can we cultivate an environment conducive to embracing joy and fostering the indwelling of the Holy Spirit within us? In the tapestry of human existence, what forms of joy hold the utmost significance and profundity?

We acknowledge that joy aligns with the desires of our Lord's heart and of the Holy Spirit. Yet, although we pray during the Liturgy that our hearts be filled with joy and grace, nevertheless, we sometimes hinder the Spirit's work in bringing joy and happiness into our lives.

Now, let us probe some internal obstacles to the cultivation of joy within our souls:

Perseverance enlarges our capacity for joy

How we perceive ourselves (and so how we perceive what is outside us) affects our capacity for joy. Some may view themselves through a lens of positivity, akin to looking through the eye of God, where hope and optimism abound. This reflects how our Lord Jesus Christ sees us, regardless of the strength of our relationship with God at any given moment. From our perspective, our Lord Christ's view of us remains unwavering. Unlike human fickleness, His love for us endures, never wavering or diminishing.

We derive this understanding from Christ's teachings in Scripture, His compassionate interactions with the weak, the sick, and the impoverished, His deliberate visits to sinners for their redemption, and His parables addressing sin. Our conviction in this truth is fortified by the writings of revered figures such as Saint Paul, Saint Peter, Saint Jude, Saint James, and the early church Fathers. Moreover, we find reassurance in the nurturing love and protective embrace of the Church, our spiritual mother. Each day spent in communion with the Church deepens our appreciation for spiritual fatherhood, a potent force within our faith community. Through this spiritual guidance, we come to witness God's unwavering love for us, a love unaltered by our actions. While He may disapprove of certain behaviours, His love for us remains steadfast. Indeed, a profound distinction exists between not liking someone and disagreeing with their actions; our Lord loves us unconditionally, just as we are.

On the other hand, some unhappily see themselves. They lack self-love and self-esteem in God, ever wanting to change something in their activity and in their personality, to change their figure perhaps. They are anxious to change their future and even their past. Such habitual dissatisfactions with oneself build up thick walls that delay the work of the Holy Spirit from within.

Dissatisfaction with oneself often leads to a persistent struggle with self-forgiveness and, more importantly, self-acceptance. Despite receiving absolution and the assurance of forgiveness for our sins from God, we may find it challenging to receive that forgiveness to ourselves. Rather than fixating on our transgressions, it is crucial that we focus on the divine covering bestowed upon us through Baptism. In His infinite grace, God has not only forgiven our sins but has also elevated us to the status of sons and kings, as it is declared, "He has made us kings and priests to His God and Father" (Revelation 1:6).

Nevertheless, the lingering effects of sin can undermine our sense of worthiness despite Christ's redemptive work through repentance and forgiveness. Through the cleansing power of the blood of Christ, as Saint Paul emphasises: "The blood of Jesus Christ His Son cleanses us from all sin" (1 John 1:7), we are purified from all sin, and our transgressions are no longer held against us.

Self-punishment, stemming from the adverse effects of sin on our souls, can deeply engrain itself within us, impacting our mental and bodily health. or goodness. It reflects a low self-esteem, characterised by a fixation on our own failings rather than turning ourselves to God's boundless mercy. Intriguingly, the early desert fathers diagnosed the habit of self-punishment as a subtle manifestation of pride, keeping individuals obsessed with themselves instead of turning to God's grace. For many, this self-imposed isolation acts as a barrier, hindering the Holy Spirit's transformative work and obstructing the entry of joy into their hearts.

> THIS PERSISTENT SELF-FLAGELLATION MANIFESTS AS AN INABILITY TO FORGIVE OURSELVES, PERPETUALLY DWELLING ON OUR SHORTCOMINGS, AND FEELING UNWORTHY OF SUCCESS

The remedy for these internal obstacles lies in repentance and the practice of the Sacrament of Repentance and Confession. This sacred rite offers a profound opportunity for the soul to stand before God, accompanied by a confessional father guided by the Holy Spirit. Here, in the presence of divine mercy, the soul uncovers its sins, and the healing of spiritual wounds begins. Through this sacramental encounter, individuals are reminded that they are not in fact defined by their sins; rather, they have the power to cast off the garment of sin and be clothed in Christ, as is said in Galatians 3:27, "For as many of you as were baptized into Christ have put on Christ." In Confession, we are invited to adorn ourselves once more with the baptismal wedding garment of righteousness.

Obstacles from outside blocking joy in the soul

Worrying over the way that others view us, a preoccupation with our own "image"– this seems to have become one of the biggest obstacles to joy in our soul, especially with our younger generation. This is the message of social media: You must constantly seek approval and popularity; only the endorsement from others makes us into something, and so we must compromise our own integrity to win the approval of the right crowd. Saint Paul's words in 1 Corinthians are amazingly effective here: "But with me it is a very small thing that I should be judged by you or by a human court, in fact, I do not even judge myself" (1 Corinthians 4:3). Here, Saint Paul underscores the insignificance of others' opinions in shaping his self-worth and identity. His steadfast commitment to prioritizing God's approval more than anything else serves us as a powerful example.

Just as with Saint Paul, their judgments hold little sway over our inner sense of joy and fulfilment. While external opinions may at times inflict hurt and undermine our inner peace, aligning ourselves with God's purpose for our lives allows us to transcend these fleeting concerns and to find enduring contentment in His divine love and acceptance.

WHEN OUR FOCUS SHIFTS TOWARDS GOD ALONE, AND WE PLACE OUR COMPLETE TRUST IN HIS SOVEREIGNTY AND GLORY, THE OPINIONS OF OTHERS DIMINISH IN SIGNIFICANCE.

Making comparisons, one aspect of this issue has become pervasive in modern life and presents a significant challenge. This tendency to compare ourselves, our achievements, and to compare even our spiritual communities can infiltrate various aspects of our lives, including our engagement with religious services and our perceptions of church leaders and ministries. However, it is crucial to recognise that attaching excessive importance to others' opinions fosters an environment ripe for comparison, resentment, and discontent.

To navigate this obstacle, we must prioritise God's perspective more than anyone or anything else. His view of us, rooted in unconditional love and divine wisdom, holds paramount significance. By anchoring ourselves in God's truth and embracing our unique journey and calling, we can safeguard against the pitfalls of comparison and find solace in His unwavering acceptance and affirmation.

When we do not enjoy what we have

Another external obstacle is to become too busy to enjoy anything in our life. When Jacob gathered all his children in Genesis 49, "Jacob called his sons and said, 'Gather together, that I may tell you what shall befall you in the last days'" (Genesis 49:1). In this chapter, he describes each of his sons. When he described Issachar, he said about him, "Issachar is a strong donkey, lying down between two burdens, He saw that rest was good, and that the land was pleasant; he bowed his shoulder to bear a burden, and became a band of slaves" (Genesis 49:14-15). Jacob describes Issachar as being under the yoke of life, daily responsibilities, success, pleasures, the world, transporting his children from one place to another, being like a windmill, the output greater than the input, to the extent that there is no time to sit and review oneself, no time to pray, no time to read the scriptures, all their dreams in life are worldly. Issachar is likened to a donkey. Such a person may be extremely rich, elite, of high academic standing, a professional, yet can still fall under the yoke of life. How, then, can such a person gain inner joy? How can the Holy Spirit work within such a person to grant them inner joy?

When we find ourselves trapped in the relentless cycle of life's demands, obligations, and worldly pursuits, akin to the burdened state of Issachar described by Jacob, it can be very difficult to cultivate inner joy. Despite external achievements and accolades, there remains a void within—a yearning for spiritual fulfilment and genuine contentment.

To break free from this cycle and invite the Holy Spirit to infuse our lives with joy, we must first acknowledge the imbalance in our lives and prioritise our spiritual well-being. Just as Issachar recognized the value of rest and the pleasantness of the land, we, too, must pause amidst life's busyness to seek moments of reflection, prayer, and spiritual nourishment.

Finding joy amid life's burdens requires a shift in perspective—a conscious choice to align our aspirations with God's purposes and to derive fulfilment from His presence rather than worldly achievements alone. By submitting our burdens and ambitions to God, we open ourselves to His transformative work within us, allowing the Holy Spirit to illuminate our path with inner joy and spiritual abundance.

Inner joy is not contingent upon external circumstances or worldly success but is rooted in our relationship with God and the realisation of His boundless love and grace. As we embrace a stance of humility, submission, and spiritual receptivity, the Holy Spirit can work wonders within us, leading us into a deeper experience of joy that transcends the fleeting pleasures of the world.

In times of confusion, uncertainty and upheaval, fear and anxiety can often grip our hearts, overwhelming us with worry and doubt. While these feelings are natural, they can escalate to unhealthy levels, paralysing us and hindering our ability to experience inner peace and joy. The recent global pandemic, COVID-19, serves as a stark reminder of how fear can become all-consuming if left unchecked.

Anchor yourself in God's unshakable promise

To combat the grip of fear and anxiety, we must anchor ourselves in the unwavering promises of our Lord Jesus Christ. These promises serve as beacons of hope amid darkness, guiding us through life's storms with assurance and trust. Our beloved Father Marcos Tawfik has compiled a remarkable booklet outlining God's promises—a testament to His faithfulness and unending love for His children.

Among the countless promises of God, several specifically address our fears: "Do not fear, little flock" (Luke 12:32), "I am with you always, even to the end of the age" (Matthew 28:20), "I will be with you. I will not leave you nor forsake you. Be strong and of good courage" (Joshua 1:5), "The angel of the Lord encamps all around those who fear Him and delivers them" (Psalm 34:7). These assurances remind us that God is our ever-present refuge and strength, offering protection and deliverance in times of distress.

The Psalms, especially, are replete with promises that bolster our faith and dispel our fears. Like David facing Goliath or Noah building the Ark, As Pope Shenouda aptly stated, we are invited to enter the ark of God's promises, finding shelter and security in His unfailing word.

WE ARE CALLED TO TRUST WHOLEHEARTEDLY IN GOD'S PROMISES, KNOWING HE IS FAITHFUL TO FULFIL THEM.

With steadfast faith and unwavering trust, let us boldly declare, "I have been young, and now am old; Yet I have not seen the righteous forsaken" (Psalm 37:25). Our Lord desires hearts fortified by the assurance of His presence and provision. Therefore, let us cast aside our fears and embrace the abundant life He offers, knowing that He who is with us is more significant than any challenge we may face. As Elisha prayed for his servant, may our eyes be opened to see the omnipotent hand of God working on our behalf, dispelling fear, and ushering in His peace.

It happened that Abba Moses was struggling with the temptation of fornication. Unable to endure his cell any longer, he went to tell Abba Isidore. The old man exhorted him to return to his cell. But he refused, saying, 'Abba, I cannot.'

Then Isidore took him out on the terrace and said to him, 'Look to the west.' He looked and saw **a crowd of demons flying about and making a ruckus, about to launch an**

attack. Then Isidore said to him, 'Now look to the east.' He turned about and saw **a countless host of holy angels shining in glory.**

Isidore said, 'You see, these are sent by the Lord to the saints to help them, while those in the west fight against them. **They who are with us are more in number than those who are against us** (2 Kg 6:16).' Then Abba Moses gave thanks to God, plucked up his courage, and returned to his cell.

—Benedicta Ward (tr.), The Sayings of the Desert Fathers (Kalamazoo: Cistercian Studies, 1975), 138.]

Indeed, these external obstacles serve to disrupt the sacred work of the Holy Spirit within us, hindering the flow of joy into our hearts. Nevertheless, through awareness and prayerful reflection, we can begin to recognize and overcome these barriers. Let us open our eyes to discern where we stand and what impedes the Holy Spirit's transformative work in our lives.

May our hearts be receptive to the gentle promptings of the Spirit, guiding us towards a deeper understanding of ourselves and a greater openness to joy. May we invite the Holy Spirit to illuminate the areas of our lives where obstacles lurk and grant us the courage and strength to address them?

As we embark on this journey of self-discovery and spiritual growth, may God's abounding love and grace overflow within us, filling our hearts with true and lasting joy. Let us submit our burdens and concerns to the Lord, trusting in His unfailing mercy and provision. May the joy of the Holy

Spirit reign in our hearts, transforming us from within and radiating God's love to all those around us.

Final words

In this chapter, we have explored various obstacles that hinder the experience of joy in our lives, both internally and externally. Through reflection on Scripture, the teachings of revered figures, and insights from our own experiences, we have identified key barriers such as habits of self-perception, constant self-dissatisfaction, making personal comparisons, and socially motivated fear. However, amidst these challenges, we have also discovered pathways to cultivate joy and foster the indwelling of the Holy Spirit within us. By anchoring ourselves in God's unwavering love, embracing the sacraments, and trusting in His promises, we can transcend the limitations of our human condition and experience the true and lasting joy that emanates from our relationship with Him.

Questions for self-reflection:

1. How do you perceive yourself, and how does this perception affect your capacity for joy?

2. In what ways do external factors, such as societal expectations and comparisons, affect your inner sense of joy?

3. Reflect on a time when you felt burdened by life's demands and responsibilities. How did you navigate through those challenges, and what role did faith play in finding inner joy?

4. How do you respond to feelings of fear and anxiety in your life? Are there specific promises of God that you find comforting during times of distress?

5. What steps can you take to cultivate a deeper relationship with God and foster the indwelling of the Holy Spirit, thereby experiencing greater joy in your life?

These reflection questions invite us to delve deeper into our spiritual journey, discerning the obstacles that hinder our joy and exploring practical steps to overcome them. As we continue to seek God's presence and guidance, may His boundless love and grace illuminate our path, leading us into a life of abundant joy and fulfilment in Him.

Chapter 16

Cultivating true Joy — the way of Humility, Prayer and Repentance

One of the brethren once asked me, "Tell us about one of the scenes you have sighted so that we can profit from it." In response I said, "Anyone who is a sinner like me does not have scenes to recount. But if you want to see a glorious scene that can truly benefit you, I can tell you where to find it. It is that of a man humble of heart and pure. This is a scene more splendid than any because through it you can see God who cannot be seen! Do not ask about a scene greater than this." Saint Pachomius the Great.

A captivating true story

Let us begin this chapter with a captivating story that really happened!

Once upon a time, in a remote corner of the world, in a country devoid of churches and far from the comfort of familiar spiritual surroundings—one of those countries where practising Christianity is prohibited by law, with no Christian meetings, no Bibles, an absolute drought of any spiritual nourishment—there lived a young man whose heart burned with an insatiable hunger for God's presence. This man, a close friend of mine, found himself in a predicament where the nearest church was a gruelling three-hour plane journey away.

Undeterred by the distance and undiminished in his devotion, he longed for Holy Communion with the divine, yearning for the nourishment of God's righteousness. With no Bible to turn to, he sought solace in the Psalms, drawing inspiration from the words that echoed through his soul, (Psalm 63:1).

> ✵
> "Early I will seek You,
> my soul thirsts for You"

Day after day, he poured out his heart in fervent prayer, immersing himself in a sacred dialogue with the Almighty. Moments turned into hours, and still, he persisted, his spirit ablaze with an unquenchable thirst for a divine encounter. "Lord," he cried, his voice trembling with longing, "I am thirsty, I am hungry, I am eager to see You, to eat You, to touch You and to be comforted by you."

Cultivating true Joy—the way of Humility, Prayer and Repentance

And then, in a moment that would forever be etched and forever engraved in his memory, the room was bathed in a radiant, pure white light, not of this world. As he blinked in awe, he beheld a sight transcending earthly comprehension. Standing before him, with wounds that bore witness to the depths of love, stood the Lord Jesus Himself. In awe and reverence of this captivating scene, he bowed down and knelt before our Lord Jesus Christ at His feet, gazing, gasping, and being taken by the depth of his wounds. His presence, a tangible manifestation of grace and mercy, filled the room, enveloping the seeker in a divine, unsurpassed, joyful embrace. He wished that time could freeze and that joy last forever.

In that sacred encounter, time seemed to stand still as the man's heart overflowed with a profound sense of awe and reverence. The hunger and thirst that had consumed him were quenched in the presence of the One who had heard his cries and answered his prayers. In that moment, he knew that God, in His infinite love, was ever beckoning His children to seek Him, to hunger and thirst for the fullness of His glory, and to savour His presence.

This captivating story serves as a potent reminder that no distance or physical limitation can hinder the hope and longing for a genuine connection with the divine. It is an invitation to us all to own the hunger and thirst within our souls, to seek God with unrelenting passion, and to trust that He will reveal Himself in the most unexpected and extraordinary ways.

May this true story inspire and encourage you to embark on your own spiritual journey, to cultivate a hunger and thirst for God that transcends any earthly boundaries, and to discover the boundless joy of communion with the divine.

As we approach the end of the journey of this book, "You Shall Surely Rejoice," we reflect on the fundamental elements that foster joy and influence the work of the Holy Spirit within us. In our previous discourse, we delved into the obstacles that hinder joy in our souls. Now, we shift our focus to the practices and influences that bring joy into our hearts and nurture the Spirit's transformative work.

In our spiritual journey, certain constants serve as the bedrock of our joy—the original prescription we refer to as the commandment of grace. Undoubtedly, we experience joy when we engage in prayer, immerse ourselves in the word of God, participate in the sacraments, especially Holy Communion, embrace repentance, extend service to others, and help the needy. These acts of devotion and service not only bring joy into our own lives but also contribute to the flourishing of joy within our communities and beyond.

As we continue to walk in the path of faith, let us remain steadfast in our commitment to these practices, allowing them to deepen our connection with God and cultivate a spirit of joy that transcends fleeting circumstances. May the Holy Spirit guide and empower us as we seek to embody the joyous life that God intends for each of us. Through unwavering faith and obedience to His commandments of grace, may we be vessels of His love and bearers of His joy to a world in need.

God's promise proclaims the essence of spiritual renewal and restoration

In the second book of Chronicles 5:13-14, we witness a special moment in Israel's history as King Solomon completes the construction of the Temple, fulfilling God's promise to his father, King David. As the priests enter the sanctuary with the ark of the covenant, a grand celebration ensues, marked by sacrifices and praises to God. The unity of the priests in worship is so fervent that the glory of the Lord fills the Temple, rendering it impossible for them to continue their ministerial duties.

King Solomon, in awe of God's presence, acknowledges the fulfilment of God's promise and blesses the assembly of Israel. He offers a prayer of dedication, expressing ten requests to God, including a plea for God's continuous presence in the Temple and forgiveness for the people's sins. King Solomon emphasises the importance of repentance and prayer, recognising God's sovereignty and his willingness to forgive His people when they turn back to Him.

Following Solomon's prayer, fire descends from heaven, consuming the burnt offerings and sacrifices, signifying God's acceptance (2 Chronicles 7). The glory of the Lord fills the Temple, and the people are overwhelmed with reverence, bowing down in worship. God reassures King Solomon of His favour, affirming that His eyes and ears will always be attentive to the prayers offered in the Temple.

This narrative underscores the significance of worship, repentance, and prayer in the corporate life of God's people. It highlights the importance of seeking God's presence and forgiveness, acknowledging His sovereignty, and committing to a life of obedience and devotion. As King Solomon's prayer is answered with divine manifestations, it serves as a testament to God's faithfulness and His responsiveness to the prayers of His people.

Then God gave a promise in one of the most important verses of Scripture. If there is nothing else you remember from this whole series, memorise this verse, which is the key, not only for joy, but for everything, to gain a stable, balanced, and steady life. Take this verse as a law in your life. God said to Solomon, "If My people who are called by My name will humble themselves, and pray and seek My face, and turn from their wicked ways, then I will hear from heaven, and will forgive their sin and heal their land" (2 Chronicles 7:14).

In 2 Chronicles 7:14, God delivers a profound promise that encapsulates the essence of spiritual renewal and restoration. This verse serves as a timeless blueprint for attaining divine forgiveness, healing, and restoration, not only for individuals but also for nations.

God's instruction is clear and concise: humility, prayer, seeking His presence, and repentance are the pathways to divine intervention and restoration. Prayer becomes a conduit for communion with the divine, a means of seeking God's guidance, wisdom, and mercy. To seek God's face means a deep longing for intimacy with the

THROUGH HUMILITY, INDIVIDUALS ACKNOWLEDGE THEIR DEPENDENCE ON GOD AND RECOGNISE HIS SOVEREIGNTY.

Creator, a desire to align one's heart and will with His divine purpose. Turning from wicked ways signifies genuine repentance and a commitment to forsake sin and pursue righteousness.

In response to such heartfelt devotion and obedience, God promises to hear from heaven, to forgive sin, and to bring healing to the land. This assurance speaks to the transformative power of God's grace and mercy, extending not only to individuals but also to communities and nations. It emphasises revival and spiritual renewal as foundational to societal well-being and prosperity.

If we as believers internalise and apply the principles outlined in (2 Chronicles 7:14), it can lead to a life marked by spiritual vitality, resilience, and fulfilment. By embracing humility, prayerfulness, and repentance, we can experience the fullness of God's forgiveness, healing, and restoration in our lives and communities. This verse serves as a beacon of hope and a reminder of God's unwavering faithfulness to those who earnestly seek Him.

To humble ourselves. Humility indeed serves as the cornerstone of our spiritual journey, the gateway to divine grace and restoration. It is a virtue revered by the saints and emphasized throughout sacred texts. It lays the groundwork for a life submission to God's will. In the words of Scripture, "God opposes the proud but gives grace to the humble" (James 4:6).

It requires us to set aside pride and self-reliance, yielding to God's wisdom and guidance in all aspects of life. True humility is not rooted in self-deprecation or a sense of worthlessness but rather in an honest appraisal of our strengths and weaknesses, considering God's infinite goodness and mercy.

HUMILITY BEGINS WITH A RECOGNITION OF OUR UTTER DEPENDENCE ON GOD, ACKNOWLEDGING HIS SOVEREIGNTY AND OUR INHERENT LIMITATIONS.

In humbling ourselves before God, we open the door for His grace to flow into our lives, transforming our hearts and circumstances. It is a posture of receptivity, allowing God to work in and through us for His glory. Humility also fosters a spirit of compassion and empathy towards others, as we recognise the dignity and value inherent in every individual created in the image of God.

In times of trial and adversity, humility enables us to submit our worries and fears into God's hands, trusting in His providence and unfailing love. It empowers us to persevere with faith and resilience, knowing that God's strength is made perfect in our weakness.

Let us then heed the call to humility and embrace it as the foundation of our spiritual lives. May we humbly submit ourselves to God's will, seeking His face earnestly in prayer and turning away from pride and self-centeredness. If we do so, we open ourselves to the abundant blessings and transformative power of God's grace, and so find true joy, peace, and victory in His presence.

Three heavyweight sins: pride, hypocrisy, and ingratitude

The Scriptures indeed highlight the gravity of these three sins, pride, hypocrisy, and ingratitude—and show their detrimental effects on our relationship with God and others. Let us mark each of these sins and their consequences:

1. Pride: Pride is often regarded as the root of all sin, manifesting itself in an exaggerated sense of self-importance and a refusal to acknowledge God's sovereignty. It led to Satan's rebellion against God and his subsequent fall from grace. Pride blinds us to our own faults and inhibits genuine repentance and humility before God. Scripture warns, "Pride goes before destruction, and a haughty spirit before a fall" (Proverbs 16:18). The consequence of pride is often a separation from God's presence and a loss of His favour.

2. Hypocrisy: Hypocrisy is to profess beliefs or virtues that one neither holds deeply nor embodies in practice. Jesus vehemently condemned the hypocrisy of the religious leaders of His time, denouncing their outward displays of piety while harbouring corrupt intentions and actions. Hypocrisy saps the integrity of our witness and empties our credibility as ambassadors of Christ. Jesus warned, "Woe to you, scribes and Pharisees, hypocrites! For you are like whitewashed tombs which indeed appear beautiful outwardly, but inside are full of dead men's bones and all uncleanness" (Matthew 23:27). The

consequence of hypocrisy is spiritual blindness and judgment.

3. A lack of gratitude: Ingratitude or thanklessness is the failure to acknowledge and appreciate the blessings bestowed upon us by God. It reflects a sense of entitlement and a lack of humility before the Giver of all good gifts. Throughout Scripture, God's people are exhorted to offer thanksgiving and praise for His abundant mercies and provisions. Failure to do so demonstrates a heart hardened to God's grace and provision. The Apostle Paul admonishes, *"In everything give thanks; for this is the will of God in Christ Jesus for you"* (1 Thessalonians 5:18). The consequence of ingratitude is a loss of blessings and an erosion of spiritual sensitivity.

Indeed, true peace and joy cannot flourish in hearts and lives tainted by sin and hypocrisy. As we engage in self-examination, let us do so honestly and sincerely, recognising the areas in our lives where we have fallen short and acknowledging our need for God's forgiveness and grace.

Let us not deceive ourselves with a façade of righteousness, attempting to cover up our inner hollowness and compromise with outward displays of good works or pious practices. Such hypocrisy only serves to deepen the divide between us and God, hindering the flow of His peace and joy into our lives.

Instead, let us humbly confess our sins before God, seeking His forgiveness and renewal.

As we remove our masks of hypocrisy and pretence, may the fragrance of Christ's love and grace permeate our lives, bringing true peace and joy that can only be found in Him. Let us invite the Holy Spirit to cleanse and purify us so that we may be vessels of honour, reflecting His glory to the world around us.

> ✳
>
> MAY WE STRIVE TO LIVE LIVES OF INTEGRITY AND AUTHENTICITY, ALLOWING GOD TO TRANSFORM OUR HEARTS AND MINDS FROM THE INSIDE OUT.

Humbling ourselves before our Lord

Let us lay ourselves bare before Him, rebuking our hearts and exposing our weaknesses to Him. Sometimes fittingly harsh words are followed later by sweetness.

Let us repent and be purified before leaving this world, or we will not enter heaven or see any joy on earth without God's help.

Let us plead with our Lord for help.

Be intent, with all our hearts, all our strength, all our will and all our mind to rid ourselves of sin.

May God grant us true repentance, not just the intention. Many times we have had good intentions of changing our ways, at New Year's Eve, for example, we made many promises and cries, but then we returned to our wicked deeds. Offer repentance for ourselves and our families and loved ones, for our ignorance and our sins. Then the Lord will hear from heaven, forgive us, heal us, and give us the peace and joy which we have been looking for and could not find for a long time. You will find joy and peace; you will no longer be afraid or anxious. The Lord will rebuild the relationship between you and Him. The Lord said, "Get up, sanctify the people, and say, because thus says the Lord God of Israel: 'There is an accursed thing in your midst, O Israel'" (Joshua 7:13).

The world will give us as much money as we want to invest in land, houses, and cars, but His Kingdom deploys completely different measures. We can amuse all people, but we will never be able to persuade our Lord, "He who keeps Israel shall neither slumber nor sleep" (Psalm 121:4).

This is the essential key to experiencing the joy in our lives: that we humble ourselves, expose our sins and turn away from them, that we seek His face, obey God, and He will grant his grace. Let us say like Job did, "I have sinned, and perverted what was right" (Job 33:27).

Final words:

In conclusion, cultivating Christian joy is intricately tied to the practices of humility, prayer, and repentance. These essential elements form the foundation upon which true joy flourishes in our lives. Through humility, we acknowledge our dependence on God and open ourselves to His transformative grace. Prayer becomes our means of communion with the divine, guiding us in seeking God's presence and will. Repentance leads to restoration and renewal as we turn away from sin and embrace God's forgiveness.

Questions for self-reflection:

1. How can I cultivate a deeper sense of humility in my daily life, recognising God's sovereignty and acknowledging my dependence on Him?

2. How can I address my prayer life to foster a deeper connection with God and seek His guidance and presence more earnestly?

3. What areas of my life require repentance and transformation, and how can I actively pursue renewal through genuine repentance?

4. How is pride, hypocrisy, or ingratitude manifested in my thoughts, words, or actions, and what steps can I take to address these areas of sin?

5. In what ways can I authentically express gratitude for God's blessings and cultivate a spirit of thankfulness in my life?

By engaging in sincere self-reflection and embracing the disciplines of humility, prayer, and repentance, we pave the way for God's joy to abound in our lives. May we continually seek His face, obey His commandments, and experience the fullness of His grace and peace.

Chapter 17

Joy had been hiding in the tomb

> *If death, which previously was strong, and for that reason terrible, now after the sojourn of the Saviour and the death and Resurrection of His body is despised, it must be evident that death has been brought to nought and conquered by the very Christ who ascended the Cross.* Saint Athanasius

When joy was born, and death was buried

We are travelling back in time to Bethany, a small village about 3 kilometres east of Jerusalem on the south-eastern slopes of the Mount of Olives. The three siblings Mary, Martha, and Lazarus lived in this village, nestled amidst rolling hills and blooming flowers. They were known for their unwavering loyalty and deep love for their friend,

Jesus, and for their hospitality to him, whenever he was down from Galilee, or up from the Jordan valley. And Jesus, in his turn, loved this family.

One fateful day, Lazarus fell gravely ill. Mary and Martha, filled with worry and desperation, sent word to our Lord Jesus, pleading for him to come and heal their ailing brother. They knew that Jesus possessed a divine power capable of miracles beyond human comprehension. With hopeful hearts, they awaited his arrival. Days passed, as Lazarus grew weaker and weaker and finally died and was buried in a tomb outside Bethany.

Mary and Martha clung to their faith, trusting that Jesus would come to their aid. And on the fourth day, their prayers were answered. Jesus came to Bethany, His presence radiating with love and compassion. As our Lord Jesus approached the tomb where Lazarus had been laid to rest, a mixture of grief and anticipation hung heavily in the air. The villagers had gathered around, their eyes filled with tears, their hearts burdened with sorrow. But little did they know that a moment of profound joy was about to unfold before their very eyes.

The tomb had been sealed for days. At our Lord's bidding, the people moved the stone covering the tomb. In a voice resonant with divine authority, He commanded, "Lazarus, come forth!" And in an instant, a moving figure could be seen in the dark opening of the tomb. The crowd gasped in astonishment as Lazarus emerged trailing graveclothes, his once lifeless body now filled with vitality and renewed spirit.

Joy had been hiding in the tomb

As Lazarus emerged from the tomb, the villagers stood in stunned silence, their eyes widening in disbelief. Time seemed to stand still momentarily as the reality of what they were witnessing sank in. Then, a collective gasp of astonishment rippled through the crowd, followed by a resounding cheer of jubilation. Tears of sorrow turned into tears of joy as the villagers witnessed the miracle unfolding before their very eyes. A wave of euphoria swept through the crowd. Joy and awe intermingled as they realised the magnitude of Jesus' power and the depth of his love. The once sombre atmosphere transformed into a scene of pure celebration. Laughter, shouts of praise, and cries of sheer happiness filled the air. The villagers could not help but embrace one another, their hearts overflowing with gratitude and wonder. They danced, sang, and rejoiced together, their voices harmonising into a chorus of thanksgiving.

> ❋
>
> AT THAT MOMENT, JOY WAS BORN, AND DEATH WAS BURIED. HOPE AROSE BRIGHTER THAN THE SUN. DESPAIR WAS DOOMED AND DARKENED FOREVER!

At that moment, the joy that flooded the villagers was palpable. It radiated from their faces, their smiles stretching from ear to ear. They could not help but share the news of Lazarus' resurrection with everyone they met, the joy spreading like wildfire throughout the village. The sight of Lazarus, lately dead but now alive, kindled a flame of hope and faith in the hearts of the villagers. They witnessed firsthand the power of Jesus, and their belief in him deepened.

The miracle became a living testimony, a reminder that The villagers celebrated long into the night. The memory of that day when Lazarus emerged from the tomb would forever be etched in their minds as a testament to the miraculous power of Jesus and the boundless joy that can be found in his presence.

EVEN IN THE DARKEST OF TIMES, JOY CAN BURST FORTH LIKE A BEACON OF LIGHT.

Mary and Martha, who had been weighed down by grief, now embraced their resurrected brother, tears of joy streaming down their faces. Joy became the anthem of Bethany as people danced, sang, and praised the name of Jesus.

Amid this celebration, Jesus stood, his eyes filled with compassion and love. He had not only brought Lazarus back from the clutches of death but had also kindled a flame of joy in the hearts of the villagers. The miracle of Lazarus' resurrection became a testament to the power of faith and the boundless love of God. And so, the story of Jesus, Mary, Martha, and Lazarus became a tale of unwavering faith, profound love, and the uncontainable joy that can be found amid life's direst hours.

Jesus interpreted the event to them, his words encircling it with a ribbon that would forever challenge all powers, physics, logic, and surpass all understanding. This ribbon would forever empower unwavering faith in the heart of every believer, infuse the undefeated words that would come from the mouth of every preacher and give solace and comfort to every troubled soul that has lost a loved one. With a voice filled with authority and love, He declared, "I am the resurrection and the life. He who believes in Me, though he may die, he shall live." (John 11:25)

As these words of holy power echoed through the crowd, a hush fell over the villagers. In that moment, they understood that Lazarus' resurrection was not just one miraculous event for them but a profound revelation of who Jesus truly was. He himself was the fountain of life and the embodiment of undying hope. The ribbon that Jesus wound around this event was the promise of everlasting life. It was a declaration that death had been conquered and that through faith in Him, all could experience a newness of life that transcended the limitations of this world. It was a bow that tied together the threads of hope, faith, and love, weaving a tapestry of divine grace. With this final word, the villagers realised that the resurrection of Lazarus was not about a temporary respite from death but a glimpse into the eternal reality that awaited them.

Jesus had unveiled the ultimate truth—the through Him, they could have abundant and everlasting life. From that day forward, the villagers clung to these words, cherishing them as a precious gift. They carried with them the message of Jesus' resurrection and the promise of eternal life and shared it with others near and far. This truth transformed their lives, and they lived with a renewed sense of purpose, knowing that through Jesus, death had lost its sting. The ribbon of Jesus' declaration would forever adorn their hearts, reminding them of the extraordinary power and depth of His love. It served as a constant reminder that even in the face of death, there was hope, there was resurrection, and there was life everlasting.

And so, the story of Lazarus' resurrection became more than a historical event. It became a beacon of hope for all generations to come. The villagers would forever hold in their hearts the belief that through Jesus, they had been given the greatest gift of all - the gift of eternal life, which is our ultimate joy, my dear reader! Yes, joy and sorrow can coexist

Show us the holy Joy of Your Resurrection!

The prayer, "Show us the holy Joy of Your Resurrection," which concludes each day of the Holy Week and Pascha rituals, fills believers with hope as they look towards Christ's crucifixion and the mercy it brings.

"Jesus Christ, our true God, willingly accepted suffering and death on the Cross for our sake. May He bring the Holy Pascha to completion with peace and reveal to us the Joy of His Resurrection."

Our church, guided by the Holy Spirit, wisely places this prayer at a time when our souls need it most. For those who love Christ in Spirit and Truth, the Holy Week and Pascha rituals are no mere commemorations but a real and profound participation in Christ's suffering, death, and resurrection.

Yet, who can genuinely bear what Christ endured for us? As the prophet Isaiah said: "He was wounded for our transgressions, He was bruised for our iniquities; the chastisement for our peace was upon Him, and by His stripes we are healed" (Isaiah 53:5-6). Saint Paul's words echo in our hearts: "He who knew no sin was made to be sin for us" (2 Corinthians 5:21), and the giver of life was sentenced to death. This was the reality of Christ's agony. Even Saint Peter, who loved Him dearly, denied Him at the first threat, and all the other disciples fled, failing to endure the pain of the Cross without the perspective of resurrection.

Understanding the weakness of human nature under the weight of despondency, our church prays, "Show us the Joy of Your Resurrection," expanding our scope of hope and lifting our spirits. This prayer reminds us that despite the intensity of Holy Week—its long prayers, solemn hymns, and contrite atmosphere—there is always a joyful expectation of resurrection.

The Holy Joy of the Resurrection, as expressed in Psalm 51:12, "Restore to me the joy of Your salvation" and by the Virgin Mary, "my spirit has rejoiced in God my Savior" (Luke 1:47), is the same joy announced to the shepherds at Jesus' birth: "I bring you good tidings of great joy" (Luke 2:10). It is the joy Christ foretold to His disciples to sustain them through His crucifixion, and the joy felt by the repentant prodigal son. This joy, granted to humanity when Christ took Barabbas' place, starts on Resurrection Day and extends throughout our lives.

The joy of the resurrection of Christ is for believers a profound and transformative experience. It surpasses all earthly happiness because it is rooted in the victory over sin and death that Jesus achieved through His resurrection.

In the early church, Christians radiated this joy, peace, and serenity to all they encountered.

The Holy Joy of the Resurrection, the triumph and victory over sin, is experienced through forgiveness and righteousness before God, purchased by Christ's sacrifice on the Cross. To procure this joy, we must put our faith in Christ's redemptive act, engage deeply with the Holy Week readings, rituals, and hymns, and approach with repentance, asceticism, spiritual struggle, and vigilance.

> ❋
> THE HOLY JOY OF THE RESURRECTION CANNOT BE LIMITED BY HUMAN EMOTIONS; IT TRANSFORMS THE CHILDREN OF GOD AS EMBODIMENTS OF JOY, PEACE, AND VICTORY OVER SIN AND DEATH.

As the Gospel of the Wise Virgins is read on Holy Tuesday, it reminds us to be vigilant, looking forward to the dawn of the Resurrection. We pray that we may be sons of light and day, never ceasing to await and to witness the Joy of Christ's Resurrection.

This joy is not merely a fleeting emotion but a deep and abiding sense of hope, peace, and assurance. The resurrection of Christ brings us the assurance that our sins are forgiven and that we have been reconciled with God. It is a reminder that no matter how broken or lost we may feel, we have the opportunity to be made new and to experience the abundant life that Christ offers. This realisation fills our hearts with gratitude, awe, and an overwhelming sense of joy. The joy of the resurrection also brings hope for the future, reminding us that this life is not the end and that there is something greater awaiting us beyond the boundaries of time and space. This hope sustains us in times of trial, brings comfort in times of grief, and encourages us to persevere in the face of adversity.

IT ASSURES US THAT DEATH IS NOT THE FINAL WORD BUT RATHER A GATEWAY TO ETERNAL LIFE IN THE PRESENCE OF GOD.

Furthermore, the joy of the resurrection compels us to share the good news with others. It is a joy that cannot be contained but overflows, urging us to share the hope and love of Christ with those around us. This joy inspires acts of compassion, service, and kindness as we seek to reflect the love and joy that we have received from Christ. In summary, the joy of the resurrection of Christ is a deep and transformative experience that fills our hearts with hope, assurance, and gratitude. It is a joy that surpasses all earthly happiness and sustains us in all circumstances.

Final words:

In Bethany, a small village near Jerusalem lived three siblings: Mary, Martha, and Lazarus. When Lazarus fell gravely ill, his sisters sent for their friend Jesus, known for His miraculous power. Despite their faith, Lazarus died and was buried before our Lord Jesus Christ arrived. Four days later, Jesus came to Bethany, bringing hope and compassion. At the tomb, Jesus commanded Lazarus to rise, and he emerged alive and well. This miracle transformed the sorrow of the villagers into profound joy, illustrating the power of faith and our Lord Jesus' divine authority. The event marked a pivotal moment in their lives, infusing them with enduring hope and faith in Jesus' promise of eternal life.

Joy had been hiding in the tomb

Questions for self-reflection:

1. How do you respond to moments of profound sorrow or grief in your life? Reflect on your emotional reactions and coping mechanisms when faced with significant loss or hardship.

2. In what ways can faith provide hope during challenging times? Consider how your beliefs or spiritual practices help you navigate demanding situations.

3. What does the story of Lazarus teach you about patience and waiting for divine intervention? Reflect on your experiences of waiting for positive changes and how faith influences your patience.

4. How can you cultivate a sense of joy and gratitude in your daily life, even amidst challenges? Explore practical ways to maintain a positive outlook and express thankfulness regularly.

5. In what ways can you support others who are experiencing grief or hardship? Consider actions you can take to offer comfort and hope to those around you.

6. How does faith in the resurrection and in eternal life influence your perspective on mortality and life's purpose? Reflect on your beliefs about life after death and how they shape your daily actions and mindset.

7. What role does community play in your experiences of joy and sorrow? Think about how your relationships with

others impact your emotional well-being and how you share in both joy and grief.

Chapter 18

The Fulness of Joy in His Presence

"The soul that loves God has its rest in God alone. in all the paths that men walk in the world, they do not attain peace until they draw nigh to hope in God" Saint Isaac the Syrian

Do not settle for anything less

Do not settle for anything less than the joy of being in His presence! Have you ever deeply considered this and focused your heart on it? In His presence!

What keeps you and me going in this life? How can you stay focused on a higher purpose when life gives you its back and presents its harshest challenges, the kinds of distress we all wish to avoid? How can you navigate steadily and peacefully the numerous obstacles and trials that so often slow us down? How can you and I swim safely in the ocean without losing sight of the final safe shore, without getting lost in the vast, relentless ocean of life, without being pounded and tossed about by the towering, unforgiving waves?

As we draw near the end of this book's journey, please allow me to say:

DO NOT SETTLE FOR ANYTHING LESS THAN THE JOY OF BEING IN HIS PRESENCE.

In Your presence, the fullness of joy

Listen to these exultant words of the psalmist: "You will show me the path of life; In Your presence is fullness of joy; At Your right hand are pleasures forevermore" (Psalm 16:11).

To understand the meaning of "in your presence there is fullness of joy," we must review the entire context of Psalm 16, which begins with King David's petition: "Preserve me, O God, for in You I put my trust." (Psalm 16:1). The word "preserve" means "to hedge about, guard, to protect, attend to." Although it is unclear why David asks for God to preserve him, it is evident that he knows whom to take refuge in, for "My goodness is nothing apart from You" (Psalm 16:2).

This shows us that God is the ultimate source of our protection and well-being. Next, King David states that he is pleased with the "As for the saints who are on the earth, "They are the excellent ones, in whom is all my delight." (Psalm 16:3). This does not mean that King David values the saints above God or places them on the same level as

God. On the contrary, He wishes to express his complete satisfaction with the righteousness (or holiness) of the saints, which is contrasted with "Their sorrows shall be multiplied who hasten after another god" (Psalm 16:4).

To be in the company of God's people brings joy, but to be in the company of godless people multiplies sorrow. Then, in (Psalm 16:5), King David describes his satisfaction with the Lord and all that He provides: "O Lord, You are the portion of my inheritance and my cup; You maintain my lot." The Lord is not simply David's portion (or inheritance). He is his chosen portion. This is significant because King David acknowledges that only the Lord can satisfy him, so he gladly welcomes all that is received from Him.

In Psalm 16:6, David exults in what it means that You maintain my lot: "The lines have fallen to me in pleasant places; Yes, I have a good inheritance..." The "lines" here are either literal or figurative. If taken literally, then the lines are the "allotted periods and the boundaries" (Acts 17:28) of King David's dwelling place. If lines should be taken figuratively, which is probably the better interpretation, then it refers to the "pleasant places" (Psalm 16:6) and "pleasures" (verse 11) at God's right hand.

The idea is that God is King David's inheritance (cf. Romans 8:17), and he rejoices in this wonderful truth. Therefore, exulting in God as his Sovereign is the same as exulting in God as his Treasure. God is the Sovereign who holds my lot. And he uses that power to make himself my beautiful inheritance—to fence me into the pleasures of knowing him. He makes himself my treasure."

The Lord is David's refuge and portion, but He is also David's counsellor: "I will bless the Lord who has given me counsel;

My heart also instructs me in the night seasons." (Psalm 16:7). In this verse, David exalts the Lord for counselling, guiding, and directing his steps, even in the night when his mind is racing, or his soul is restless. In these moments, the Lord reassures David of His ever-abiding presence by comforting him with His Word: "Your word is a lamp to my feet and a light to my path" (Psalm 119:105; cf. Psalm 16:11). David will not be "shaken" (Psalm 16:8), abandoned (verse 9), or experience "corruption" (verse 10) because the Lord will preserve him.

We can now answer the question, what does "in your presence there is fullness of joy" mean? In the presence of God, there is hope of everlasting joy. This hope does not put us to shame since we know that God is trustworthy and faithful. "For now, we see in a mirror dimly, but then face to face. Now I know in part; then I shall know fully, even as I have been fully known" (1 Corinthians 13:12).

Therefore, we can be confident that death will not keep us from the fullness of joy in God's presence. In heaven, we will behold the radiant beauty of God's face forevermore.

"Beloved, we are God's children now, and what we will be has not yet appeared; but we know that when he appears, we shall be like him, because we shall see him as he is" (1 John 3:2). But wait a minute. How do we remain in His presence despite every our extremely jammed and crowded lifestyle that we are now living and struggling to keep our heads above the water?

The Practice of the Presence of God

Brother Lawrence of the Resurrection, a humble 17th-century monk, offers us timeless wisdom in his book, "The Practice of the Presence of God." He teaches that one can experience God's presence in the mundane and ordinary activities of daily life. For Brother Lawrence, being constantly aware of God's presence transformed his life, and brought him profound peace and joy.

"The Practice of the Presence of God" is a spiritual classic that invites us to transform our daily lives into a continuous conversation with the Divine. Brother Lawrence shares his profound yet simple approach to spirituality: living every moment in the presence of God amid life's ordinary tasks. This book tells us of his journey, in which he learned that even mundane activities like cooking in the kitchen, washing dishes, or later, sandal-making, could become acts of worship. His wisdom and practical advice offer a path to inner peace and a deeper connection with God. It makes this little book a treasured guide for anyone seeking to infuse their everyday life with sacred purpose and tranquillity.

Brother Lawrence's practice involved continual conversation with God, no matter what task he was performing. He believed that the key to spiritual life was to develop an awareness of God's presence at all times in all situations. Whether washing dishes or praying, Brother Lawrence maintained a constant dialogue with God, finding joy and contentment in His presence.

In his introduction to this timeless book, Sid Israel Roth, host of Its Supernatural! Television shares his personal journey:

"As a new believer, I read 'The Practice of the Presence of God" and realised I wanted and needed what Brother Lawrence had discovered. However, I lacked discipline and quickly gave up my pursuit. Years later, with grey hair, I revisited this remarkable book. Now, practising God's presence is my magnificent obsession. I am convinced that our purpose as believers is to walk in His love 24/7.

EVERYTHING I DO, NO MATTER HOW INSIGNIFICANT, IS FOR THE LOVE OF GOD AND PEOPLE."

"When we get to heaven, the love we deposited on earth will be our legacy. My friend Rick Joyner had an eight-hour dream where he visited heaven. Jesus told him he was granted this visitation because he used the key to eternal joy. When Rick asked what the key was, Jesus answered, "When you set your heart to bring Me pleasure above seeking your own." Rick told me he experienced a level of joy beyond anything he had known.

On another occasion, Jesus also told Rick, "I loved washing dishes with Brother Lawrence. He was my friend." Jesus longs for your friendship, too. Talk to Him constantly. He is always with you at all times."

Reflect on this beautiful book of Brother Lawrence. Imagine being in God's presence 24/7 and think about the flowing rivers of both joy and peace that will fill your heart. Imagine being with Jesus all the time and consider how this relationship can help you navigate life's challenges and obstacles.

Let us then re-evaluate any earthly attractions or possessions that sometimes lure us and reflect on whether they hold any significance compared to the joy of being with Him. Practicing the presence of God can transform our lives, filling them with profound peace and unwavering joy.

Just keep swimming!

The very colourful Disney animated movie Finding Nemo follows the adventures of Marlin, an overprotective clownfish, on his journey across the ocean to find his missing son, Nemo. Along the way, Marlin meets Dory, a friendly but forgetful fish who helps him navigate the perils of the ocean. It is a heartwarming tale of determination, love, and the power of persistence.

In all the busy events of this simple drama, there is a caption that has always resonated for me. One line in the whole tale stands out for its great strength and meaning. When Dory, the forgetful fish, keeps encouraging Marlin, the dad, to keep searching for Nemo, she simply says, "Just keep swimming." This simple yet powerful mantra encapsulates the persevering in hope that we need if we are to maintain our course in the face of life's challenges. Just "keeping swimming" means continuing to move forward, no matter how turbulent the waters become.

But how can you keep swimming despite any wave, any challenge, any obstacle? We need something above and beyond all that we face—something not of this world. We need something from above us, something we can draw and gain from being in the presence of Someone, in the presence of God.

When you remain in God's awesome and divine presence, it is like a solar panel battery exposed to direct sunlight. The panel is always fully charged without fail, continuously receiving energy and strength.

IN THE SAME WAY, BEING IN GOD'S PRESENCE PROVIDES US WITH THE CONSTANT REPLENISHMENT WE NEED TO KEEP MOVING FORWARD, NO MATTER THE TRIALS WE FACE.

In the rich journey of different colourful experiences, life has taught me that when we face life's challenges, it is not our strength that can keep us afloat, but the divine presence and assistance from above. But to experience this, we must keep swimming, like Marlin and Dory in Finding Nemo. Like the solar panel continuously receiving energy from the sunlight, we must remain in God's presence, drawing the strength to persevere through life's relentless waves until we reach our safe shore above.

My blessed sister Anna Silvas who was so kind to accept editing this book once shared the following with me "To me it is very similar to another watchword which I have brought to bear in prayer for some time now: "Just keep practicing turning to God." I think of it when I take up a round of the Jesus Prayer on the beads. I do not expect Great Internal Feelings, but simply keep-at-it-ness, for the Lord's sake. Every invocation of the Holy Name with attention, then, is practice of turning to God. So just keep at it, do not give up, "just keep swimming."

This divine connection fuels our perseverance, guiding us through the relentless waves of life toward our ultimate, safe shore, the Kingdom of God that has been prepared, secured, and promised for us. Nothing can stop us, nothing can slow us, and we will remain joyfully swimming and battling life's relentless waves.

Practices for living in His Presence

Psalm 16:11 says, "You will show me the path of life; In Your presence is fullness of joy; At Your right hand are pleasures forevermore." This verse offers profound insights into finding true joy and fulfilment through a close relationship with God. Here are practical ways to apply these teachings in daily life:

1. Seek God's Presence Daily through:

    Prayer: Dedicate time each day to prayer. Speak to God about your fears, hopes, and gratitude. Prayer is a direct line to God's presence.

    Scripture Reading: Make it a habit to read the Bible daily. Reflect on the verses and how they apply to your life. The Scriptures proclaim God's word to us, the source of guidance and joy.

    Liturgy: Take part in regular worship, both privately and during Liturgies. Chanting, meditating, and focusing on God's attributes draws you closer to Him.

2. Trust in God's Protection and Guidance by means of:

    Faith Over Fear: When facing challenges, remind yourself of King David's trust in God's protection. Rather than giving way to fear, choose to trust that God is able and all willing to guard you and to guide you.

Remembering Past Blessings: Reflect on past instances where God has protected and provided for you. Let these memories bolster your faith in His continued care.

3. Delight in God and His People through:

   Community Involvement: Surround yourself with faithful believers who encourage your faith. Participate in church activities, Bible study groups, or Christian fellowships.

   Serving Others: Find joy in serving others. Volunteer your time and talents to help those in need, which is both a reflection of God's love and a source of personal joy.

4. Make God Your Chosen Portion by:

   Prioritising God Above All: Make a conscious decision to put your relationship with God above material possessions or worldly achievements. **Letting Him be your primary source of fulfilment –** without which not.

   Gratitude and Contentment: Cultivate a heart of gratitude. Regularly thank God for His blessings and find contentment in His provisions, recognising that true satisfaction comes from Him.

5. Follow God's Counsel through:

   Seeking Wisdom: Repeatedly ask for God's wisdom in making decisions. Trust that He will guide your steps and provide the necessary insight through His Word and the Holy Spirit.

Reflecting and meditating: Take time to meditate on God's word and listen for His guidance. In moments of uncertainty, seek His direction through quiet reflection and prayer.

6. Maintain your Hope of Eternal Joy by:

    Keeping an eternal perspective. Remembering our ultimate joy, the promise of eternal life with God, helps us endure temporary hardships.

    Encouraging Yourself: When faced with trials, encourage yourself with the truth of God's promises. Remind yourself that ultimate joy and pleasure are found in His presence, both now and forevermore.

    Writing it down: Keep a spiritual journal in which you write down your prayers, reflections, and how you see God working in your life. This can help you stay connected and see His faithfulness over time, especially when the going gets tough.

    Savouring nature and solitude: spend time in nature, appreciating God's creation. Use these moments to reflect on His greatness and draw closer to Him away from daily distractions.

By integrating such practices of the presence of God into your life – and you might think of others – you can cultivate a deeper connection with God and find lasting joy, whatever the circumstances may be.

Embracing the truth of Psalm 16:11

As we conclude this chapter, I invite you to embrace the truth of Psalm 16:1: "You will show me the path of life; In Your presence is fullness of joy; At Your right hand are pleasures forevermore." This verse is not just a promise for the future but a living reality to be experienced each day. providing us with unwavering strength and hope amidst life's challenges, transforming your outlook and strengthening your faith, providing a foundation of joy and peace that endures through all of life's challenges.

Embrace the Path of Life! Take the first step towards a deeper relationship with God by intentionally seeking Him daily. Let His Word guide your decisions and actions, and trust in His plan for your life. As King David found refuge, delight, and counsel in God, so can you. Let God be your chosen portion and the source of your satisfaction.

GOD'S PRESENCE IS THE SOURCE OF ALL TRUE JOY AND FULFILMENT,

Cultivate Joy in His Presence. Make it a priority to spend time in God's presence through prayer, worship, and reflection. Remember, joy is not found in the absence of challenges but in the presence of God. When you face life's towering waves and relentless trials, anchor yourself in His love and promises. Like the unforgettable mantra, "Just keep swimming." Keep moving forward, knowing that God is with you every step of the way, offering you the fullness of joy that only He can provide.

Live with an Eternal Perspective. Keep your eyes fixed on the eternal joy awaiting you in God's presence. This world is not our final home; we are destined for a beautiful inheritance that surpasses all understanding. Let this hope inspire you to persevere, to live a life of purpose and joy, knowing that at God's right hand are pleasures forevermore.

A Cohesive Conclusion

Throughout this book, we have been exploring the profound truths of finding hope, strength, and joy in God's presence. From resilient real-life stories to the life-saving power of prayer and trust in God during our darkest moments, we have seen that His enduring presence is the key to surviving and thriving in life. Just like a rescue helicopter arriving at the perfect moment, God's presence is always timely, always sufficient, and always transformative.

Now, I encourage you, my dear reader, to take these teachings to heart. Commit to walking the path of life that God has set before you. Seek Him earnestly, delight yourself in His presence, and experience the fullness of joy that He offers for all of us who are invited to nothing less than You shall Surely Rejoice.

So, beloved reader, "just keep swimming." Keep moving forward in faith, hope, and love. Launch out into the deep of God's presence, where you find the fullness of joy and the pleasures that last forever. Let the joy of the Lord be your strength as you navigate the vast and relentless ocean of life until you find your final, safe shore in His everlasting arms.

Questions for self-reflection:

1. What does being in God's presence mean to me personally, and how do I prioritize it in my daily life?

Reflect on how you consciously seek and remain in God's presence amidst your daily activities and responsibilities.

2. When I face challenges or hardships, how do I rely on God's protection and guidance like King David did in Psalm 16? Consider moments of difficulty in your life and evaluate how you trusted in God's sovereignty during those times.

3. How can I better practice the presence of God in mundane or routine moments, as Brother Lawrence describes?

Think about the ordinary tasks of your day and how you can transform them into moments of communion with God.

4. In what ways have I made God my "chosen portion," and how can I ensure He remains my ultimate source of fulfillment?

Reflect on your desires and priorities—do they reflect a life that treasures God above all else?

5. What are some practical ways I can cultivate an eternal perspective in my life, especially when navigating life's challenges?

Reflect on how keeping your eyes fixed on eternal joy can help you persevere through current trials or obstacles.

6. How can I, like the mantra "just keep swimming," cultivate perseverance in my spiritual journey, knowing that God's presence will sustain me?

Consider how the analogy of the solar panel (drawing strength from God's presence) applies to your life and spiritual perseverance.

Chapter 19

The Joy of Being Forgiven

> *"I rejoice, not because you were grieved, but because you were grieved into repenting. For you felt a godly grief, so that you suffered no loss through us. For godly grief produces a repentance that leads to salvation without regret, whereas worldly grief produces death."* Saint Clement of Rome on 2 Corinthians 7:9–10

The transformative power of repentance and God's forgiveness

Coming to the concluding chapter of "You Surely Rejoice," I want to thank and express my gratitude to you, dear reader, for joining me on this journey seeking out joy. Throughout our exploration, we have encountered various facets of joy, but the pinnacle of this experience lies in the profound joy that accompanies repentance and forgiveness. Nothing equals or surpasses the joy poured generously into our hearts when we live and embrace the transformative power of repentance and receive God's most precious gift of forgiveness. This is the utmost fulfilment of joy that any human being, fallen and mortal, can experience, and it is given to us freely without any cost when we humble ourselves to the Lord, repenting from our sins, iniquities, and transgressions. Hence, we have chosen this theme as the concluding finale as it deeply demonstrates the pinnacle of Joy, which is granted and preserved freely for every sinner.

This joy so beautifully depicted as deeply and richly illustrated in the most glorious tableau of repentance painted in words and meticulously portrayed by Saint Luke the evangelist in his gospel chapter 15. In this chapter, joy is celebrated not only by heaven and angels but also by bringing solace and peace to our own needy souls. This parable of our Lord is a fitting conclusion to our journey since it distils the essence of true joy. Our Lord and Saviour Christ tells us "I say to you that likewise there will be more joy in heaven over one sinner who repents than over ninety-nine just persons who need no repentance" (Luke 15:7). This powerful image reminds us that our

I earnestly and humbly pray for the Holy Spirit to guide us through and that He may pour out the abundance of His joy into your life.

REPENTANCE AND FORGIVENESS HAVE A PROFOUND IMPACT, NOT ONLY ON OUR OWN LIVES HERE BELOW, BUT ALSO IN THE HEAVENLY REALM.

The joy of repentance and being forgiven is the pinnacle of that joy and peace that accompanies the believer in the entire short journey of life in this perishable world.

The liberation of being forgiven: a transforming power beyond shame

Once upon a time, in a small village nestled amidst rolling hills, there lived a woman named Photini. Her name, given by the Eastern Orthodox Church, honours her role as the Samaritan woman at the well told in the Gospel of Saint John chapter 4.

Photini carried the heavy weight of her past on her shoulders, burdened by the shame and ridicule that society had cast upon her. She had led a life filled with sinful lusts, entangled in the glamour of a world that promised pleasure, security, and happiness, but only left her feeling bitterly empty.

Every day, Photini would walk to the village well to fetch water. But unlike others, she chose the hottest hour of noon to avoid the prying eyes and judgmental whispers of her neighbours, who would visit the well in the cool of the evenings. The weight of her past actions hung heavy in the air about her. She felt trapped by the chains of her own mistakes.

One scorching day, as the sun reached its zenith, Photini found herself at the well once again. But this time, her encounter was different. A weary traveller sat by the well, seeking respite from his toilsome journey up from the Jordan Valley. It was none other than Jesus Christ himself.

Our Lord Jesus looked with fathomless compassion into Photini's eyes as she reached to draw up water. No one had ever looked at her that way before, as if seeing through and beyond her past. He saw a woman yearning for forgiveness and redemption. In their conversation, the longest recorded conversation Jesus had with anyone, he unveiled the transformative power of forgiveness.

With words filled with compassion and love, Jesus offered Photini a chance to be set free from the shackles of her sins. Overwhelmed with gratitude and with tears streaming down her face, she accepted this divine gift of forgiveness.

At that moment, as the weight of her guilt was lifted, Photini felt a surge of liberation and newfound strength. She left behind her empty water pot, symbolising her shedding the shame of her past, and embraced the courage to face the world again without fear.

Photini's transformation was remarkable. She no longer hid herself away, cowering at the judgment of others. Instead, she fearlessly proclaimed the name of Jesus Christ to all those townsfolk whom formerly she had feared, spreading the message of forgiveness and redemption to all who would listen.

Her story spread far and wide, touching the hearts of those burdened by their own mistakes and offering them hope. People began to see the transformative power of being forgiven, as Photini's life became a living testament to the grace and love of God. And because of her witness, the townsfolk came out themselves, streaming towards Christ and inviting him to their town.

And so, in the village of hills and whispers, Photini's journey of forgiveness became a beacon of light, reminding everyone that no matter how deep the shame or how heavy the burden, there is in Christ always a path towards redemption and a chance to begin anew. Her story, the longest story about a woman in the Bible, continues to inspire generations, reminding them of the transformative power of forgiveness and the boundless love of Jesus Christ.

Saint Mary The Egyptian: an atonement story of God's forgiveness.

I feel there is no stronger demonstration of genuine repentance and forgiveness than the remarkable story of one of the Saints who is very dear to my heart, Saint Mary the Egyptian. She has always been a true blessing in my life, a source of inspiration and hope in moments of weakness and despair and an enormous power and supply of Heavenly joy to me and, I believe, many people. Her story not only brings joy to my heart, but also deepens my hope in God's unlimited and unsearchable mercy for His children, even for weak sinners like me.

I am truly blessed to be a part of the Saint George Coptic Orthodox Church in Sydney, where we are fortunate to have a magnificent icon of this highly revered Saint. Every time I stand before her, I am filled with a deep sense of reverence, offering incense, gazing upon her image, and staying for a moment of meditation before her as I seek her intercession through prayer. The story of this Saint's heartfelt and profound repentance holds invaluable lessons for all of us who yearn for joy in our own lives. Whenever I pause before her icon, I find myself silently questioning her, longing to understand how she was able to undergo such a transformation. Although I do not receive a direct response, a profound sense of joy permeates my heart, soul, and mind as I continue my journey around the church raising incense.

Saint Mary of Egypt was a desert ascetic of the sixth century who, after living a life of prostitution, repented and dedicated her life to the Lord. Running away at the age of twelve from her home in Alexandria, Mary followed the passions of the body and lived as a harlot for seventeen years. She refused money from the men she engaged but survived by begging.

One day, the whole purpose for Saint Mary's earthly life suddenly changed. She met a group of young men travelling to Jerusalem in order to venerate the Holy Cross and tried to seduce them as she went with them on their journey. Once the group reached the church and went towards it, Saint Mary of Egypt was prohibited from entering by an unseen force. After three attempts, she remained outside the church, where she looked up and saw the icon of the Theotokos. She immediately began to weep and prayed to the Theotokos to allow her to see the Holy Cross. She promised that she would renounce her worldly desires and go wherever the Theotokos might lead her. After this conversion, she fled into the desert to live as an ascetic. For seventeen years, Mary was tormented by the wild beasts of "mad desires and passions," while surviving on minimal food, found in the form of scarce herbs from the land. The Theotokos helped her overcome her temptations after all those years and led her to live a righteous life.

Meanwhile, a certain elder named Zosimas lived in one of the monasteries of Palestine. He had been brought up in the monastic ways and customs and was very experienced as a monk. But he began to be tormented by the notion that he was perfect in everything and needed no further instruction from anyone. He asked himself, "Is there a monk on earth who can be of use to me and show me a kind of asceticism that I have not accomplished? Is there a man to be found in the desert who has surpassed me?" An angel of God appeared and instructed him to go to the monastery by the river Jordan. During his stay at the monastery, the monks were sent out in the desert across the Jordan to spend some time during Lent before the Divine Passion and Resurrection of Christ.

It was on this excursion into the desert that the elder Saint Zosimas came upon saint Mary the Egyptian. She called out to him by his name and asked for his cloak so that she might cover her body and ask him for a blessing. Zosimas was terrified and realized that only a person with spiritual insight could have known his name. After recounting her story to him, Mary asked Zosimas to meet her again the following year at sunset on Holy Thursday by the banks of the Jordan. A year later, Saint Zosimas did precisely this. Before he could begin to doubt the experience, Saint Mary appeared on the opposite side of the Jordan and miraculously walked across the water towards him.

She received Holy Communion from him and instructed him to return to where they first met exactly a year later. When he did so, he found Mary's body with a message written on the sand asking him for burial and revealing that she had died immediately after receiving Communion the year before. Amazed, Saint Zosima began to dig and was later joined by a lion who helped him finish the digging. After burying Saint Mary of Egypt, he returned to the monastery, told everyone of what he had witnessed, and remedied the faults of the monks there.

First Path Of Repentance

Saint John Chrysostom, in one of his beautiful and profound homilies, summarised the path that our esteemed Saint Mary the Egyptian went through in five practical steps that all of us believers are invited to practice and so experience the pinnacle of joy; the joy of repentance and being forgiven. These five paths of repentance show that conversion is a continuous journey of healing and transformation that involves contrition, prayer, forgiveness, almsgiving, and humility.

Saint John Chrysostom's outline of the five paths of repentance comes from one of his homilies, Hom. De diabolo tentatore 2, 6: PG 49, 263-264.

A first path of repentance is the condemnation of your own sins:

For this reason, too, the prophet wrote: I said: I will accuse myself of my sins to the Lord, and you forgave the wickedness of my heart (Psalm 32:5). Therefore, you too should condemn your own sins; that will be reason enough for the Lord to forgive you, for a man who condemns his own sins is slower to commit them again. Rouse your conscience to accuse yourself while you are within your own house,

BE THE FIRST TO ADMIT YOUR SINS AND YOU WILL BE JUSTIFIED.

lest it become your accuser before the judgment seat of the Lord."

Second Path Of Repentance: Forgiveness

That, then, is one exceptionally good path of repentance. Another and no less valuable path is to put out of our minds the harm done to us by our enemies, to master our anger, and to forgive our fellow servants' sins against us. Then, our own sins against the Lord will be forgiven. Thus, you have another way to atone for sin: "if you forgive your debtors, your heavenly Father will forgive you" (Matthew 6:12-14).

Third Path Of Repentance: Prayer

Do you want to know of a third path? It consists of prayer that is fervent and careful and comes from the heart.

Fourth Path Of Repentance: Almsgiving

If you want to hear of a fourth, I will mention almsgiving, whose power is great and far-reaching.

Fifth Path: Humility

If, moreover, a person lives a modest, humble life, no less than the other things I have mentioned, this too takes sin away. Proof of this is the tax-collector who had no charitable deeds to mention but offered his humility instead and was relieved of a heavy burden of sins.

Thus, I have shown you five paths of repentance: condemnation of your own sins, forgiveness of our neighbour's sins against us, prayer, almsgiving, and humility.

Walking Daily In Repentance

Do not be idle, then, but walk daily in all these paths; they are easy, and you cannot plead your poverty. For, though you live out your life amid great need, you can always set aside your wrath, be humble, pray diligently and condemn your own sins; poverty is no hindrance. (almsgiving, I mean). The widow proved that when she put her two mites into the box!

POVERTY IS NOT AN OBSTACLE TO OUR CARRYING OUT THE LORD'S BIDDING, EVEN WHEN IT COMES TO THAT PATH OF REPENTANCE, WHICH INVOLVES GIVING MONEY

Spiritual Health

Now that we have learned how to heal these wounds of ours, let us apply the cures. Then, when we have regained genuine health, we can confidently approach the holy table, go gloriously to meet Christ, the king of glory, and attain eternal blessings through the grace, mercy and kindness of Jesus Christ, our Lord.

Concluding Summary:

In this concluding chapter, we have delved into the profound joy accompanying repentance and forgiveness, recognising it as the jewel in the crown of spiritual joy.

Through the parables of repentance in Saint Luke's gospel, we have witnessed the transformative power of turning back to God and receiving His forgiveness. This chapter serves as a fitting conclusion to our exploration of joy, highlighting the essence of true spiritual fulfilment found in reconciliation with God.

As we reflect on the journey we have embarked on together, let us carry with us the profound truth that repentance and forgiveness bring unparalleled joy into our lives. May we earnestly seek to cultivate a spirit of repentance, knowing that it leads to the abundant joy that surpasses earthly pleasures.

Questions for self-reflection:

1. How has my understanding of joy matured through this journey of exploration?

2. In what ways do I personally experience the joy of repentance and forgiveness in my life?

3. What obstacles hinder me from fully embracing repentance and experiencing the joy it brings?

4. How can I cultivate a deeper sense of humility and openness to repentance in my daily life?

5. What steps can I take to extend forgiveness to others and experience the freedom and joy it brings?

6. What lessons can I draw from the story of Saint Mary the Egyptian in my own journey of seeking joy through repentance?

7. How can I integrate the insights gained from this chapter into my ongoing spiritual growth and pursuit of joy?

CLOSING WORDS

Dear reader, as we come to the end of this journey together, let us remember that joy is not merely an option but an essential companion during our earthly pilgrimage. It serves to empower us, enabling us to radiate God's eternal love to all humanity. In a world where true joy may seem scarce, we are each invited to purposefully embrace and live joyfully.

May we not be deterred by the scarcity of joyful folk around us, but whatever about that, let us at least be beacons of joy in our communities. Let us taste and experience the richness of joy that comes from walking in alignment with God's will and embracing His love.

As we continue our individual paths, may the pursuit of joy be a guiding light, leading us ever closer to God and His abundant blessings. Let us live purposefully, knowing that joy is not just a fleeting emotion but a steadfast presence that sustains us through life's trials and triumphs.

Thank you for joining me on this journey. May you be filled with the overflowing joy that comes from knowing and walking with our loving Creator.

May God bless your life, fill your life with His abundant joy, and fill the church with His peace.

Scan the QR code to go to our

website where you will find

Book reviews

Great deals

Our full library of books

www.ingramcontent.com/pod-product-compliance
Lightning Source LLC
Chambersburg PA
CBHW030852170426
43193CB00009BA/577